ADVENTURES IN
ORIENTAL COOKING

Adventures in
ORIENTAL

Delicious Dishes from
China, Japan, Korea,
Philippine Islands,
Indonesia, Southeast Asia,
India, Iran, Syria, Turkey,
and Greece

COOKING

by NOBUKO KAKINUKI

JAPAN PUBLICATIONS, INC.

Published by Japan Publications, Inc., Tokyo, Japan

Distributed by Japan Publications Trading Company
1255 Howard St., San Francisco, California 94103 U.S.A.
P.O.Box 5030, Tokyo International, Tokyo, Japan

Library of Congress Catalog Card Number 72-79646
ISBN 0-87040-002-9

First printing: May 1973

Printed in Japan

Preface

I have been working on this book for about eight years. You may wonder why it took this long to complete, but with raising five children and my poor English, it was quite a project. As you may know, I was raised in Japan. I was born near Kyoto in Shiga Prefecture, in a village next to a beautiful lake called Biwa. I was the youngest of the four children of Genshichiro and Iku Kakinuki, who were both of samurai descent. Since samurai were the highest caste in Japan's old feudal system, they ate the finest foods. The recipes for many of these were handed down to me.

My whole family was interested in cooking and good eating. I remember my mother as one of the best and most gracious of hostesses and a fine cook. She would hold large parties often, and I would watch the preparations for all the traditional dishes, especially those of the New Year celebration. My mother taught me many secrets about cooking. Rather unusually, the men in my family too were interested in cooking. My father was reputed to be an excellent cook, although I do not remember this myself: he died before I was ten months old. But my brother inherited his love of cooking. He was seventeen years older than I and was very fatherly toward me. He liked having me watch him cook, and I too greatly enjoyed it. I remember that he would tell his wife to rest on Sunday and would cook Western or Chinese dishes he had learned about on his travels before his marriage.

I met my late hasband in 1950 (he died in 1970). He was from Fall River, Massachusetts, the son of the owner of a restaurant called The Mayflower. He taught me how to cook American-style foods and desserts. We settled in a small town in the United States called Big Springs, Texas, in 1952. I shall never forget the kindness of the townspeople there. Most of them had never seen a Japanese before, and World War II had only recently ended. Yet the ladies of the town helped me orient myself to the new life style, inviting me to ladies-club meetings, tea parties, baby showers, and all the town events.

Shortly after we settled down, I had my first experience with cooking Japanese food in the United States. My husband invited his Air Force chaplain to dinner, and the chaplain requested that I cook suki-yaki because he had never tasted Japanese food and had heard from a fellow chaplain, who had been stationed in the Orient, how delicious it was. I was in a very bad situation: I couldn't find any of the ingredients I needed. A friendly Red Cross worker found some Chinese soy sauce for me, not knowing how different this is from true shoyu (Japanese soy sauce). But in the end I used it, substituted sherry for sake, and green onions, spinach, celery, and carrots for the Japanese vegetables I could not get, and sliced sirloin steak the way that sukiyaki meat is sliced. I apologized when I served the meal, but it turned out to be a great success. The chaplain and the friend he brought to dinner had never tasted anything like it, and they thought it was wonderful. They even asked if they could come again. Today none of you need find yourself in such a predicament. All the ingredients in the recipes in this book are available throughout the country in special grocery stores, whose addresses are listed in the appendix.

My husband and I were reluctant to leave friendly Big Springs, but we later settled in San Francisco. There, in 1963, I served as adult education chairman of an E.S.L. (English as a Second Language) volunteer teacher group. The students were non-English speaking parents of children at Frank McCoppin Public School and came from many places—Japan, China, Armenia, Argentina, France, Russia, Indonesia, Iran, Iraq, Taiwan, Holland, Vietnam, Korea, and Malaysia. The teachers too represented many ethnic groups, including nisei (second generation Japanese-American), who, to my great surprise, knew nothing about the Japanese cuisine. I was very happy to share Japanese and Asian cooking techniques with the nisei, and soon all of us, teachers and students alike, were sharing the recipes and cooking methods of our native lands.

In 1965, I began teaching international gourmet cooking, centered mainly on the Japanese cuisine, at the Y.W.C.A. in San Francisco. Later I started teaching classes at the new Kikkoman Cooking Center in the Japanese Cultural and Trade Center in San Francisco.

I sincerely hope that *Adventures in Oriental Cooking* will help make different peoples more friendly towards each other just as my own

experiences in teaching and learning to cook have made me more under-
standing of people from other countries.

I dedicate this book to my beautiful daughter Maria, whose interest
in cooking exceeds mine and whose help was invaluable to me. I also
thank all my friends and students for their support.

September 1972

Nobuko Kakinuki

Contents

General Introduction

One of the most interesting and rewarding activities of the homemaker is preparing food for the health and enjoyment of the family. All countries and peoples have distinctive cooking and eating habits, and in this age of mass communication there is no reason why foods from all parts of the world should not be known and enjoyed by people outside the lands that originated them. Because I believe that the foods of the Orient have much to offer the people of the West in terms of pleasure and nutrition, I have compiled this sampling of the cuisines of China, Japan, Korea, the Philippine Islands, Southeast Asia, India, and the Levant. In each section I have given several basic recipes and have added others of special interest. All of these dishes have been successfully prepared in the United States, using materials generally available.

To ensure good results I recommend that you carefully read the general information given below. It will stand you in good stead in dealing with oriental foods or with any other dishes you prepare. Standard terms and measurements are all clearly defined. Do not vary from the quantities given in the recipes for failure often results from inaccurate measuring.

A. Table of weights, measures, abbreviations and equivalents

Abbreviations	Measurement	Equivalent
—	dash	less than $\frac{1}{8}$ tsp
tsp	teaspoon	3 tsp equal 1 tbsp
tbsp	tablespoon	16 tbsp equal 1 cup
—	cup	2 cups equal 1 pint
pt	pint	2 pints equal 1 quart
qt	quart	4 quarts equal 1 gallon
lb	pound	16 oz equal 1 pound
kg	kilogram	2.2 pounds equal 1 kg

B. Table of tablespoon equivalents (to 1 cup)

Measurement	Equivalent
1 tablespoon	$\frac{1}{16}$ cup
5$\frac{1}{3}$ tablespoons	$\frac{1}{3}$ cup
8 tablespoons	$\frac{1}{2}$ cup
10$\frac{2}{3}$ tablespoons	$\frac{2}{3}$ cup
12 tablespoons	$\frac{3}{4}$ cup
14 tablespoons	$\frac{7}{8}$ cup
16 tablespoons	1 cup

C. Table of food equivalents

Food	Unit	Equivalent
Butter	1 lb	2 cups
"	1 oz	2 tablespoons
"	egg-size piece	1$\frac{1}{2}$ ounces
Flour	1 lb	4 cups sifted
"	1 oz	4 tablespoons
Cake flour	1 lb	4$\frac{1}{2}$ cups sifted
Cornmeal	1 lb	3 cups
Sugar, brown	1 lb	2$\frac{3}{4}$ cups packed
Sugar, granulated	1 lb	2 cups
Sugar, powdered	1 lb	4$\frac{3}{4}$ cups sifted
Milk	1 cup	$\frac{1}{4}$ cup dried milk plus 1 cup water
"	1 cup	$\frac{1}{2}$ cup evaporated milk plus $\frac{1}{2}$ cup water
Sour milk	1 cup	1 cup milk plus 1 tablespoon vinegar (let stand 30 minutes)
Baking powder	$\frac{1}{2}$ tsp	1 egg white
Soda	$\frac{1}{2}$ tsp	2 teaspoons baking powder
Chocolate	1 oz	2 tablespoons
Chocolate	1 oz	3 tablespoons cocoa plus 1 tablespoon butter
"	1 oz	1 square
Cocoa	1 lb	4 cups

Food	Unit	Equivalent
Cocoa	1 oz	4 tablespoons
Rice	1 cups raw	3 cups, cooked
Rice	1 lb	2 cups, raw
Egg	1 lb	9 average-size eggs
Salt	$\frac{1}{8}$ tsp	a pinch with 2 fingers
"	$\frac{1}{4}$ tsp	a pinch with 3 fingers

D. Emergency substitutions

Ingredient	Substitute
1 tablespoon cornstarch	2 tablespoons flour (approx)
1 whole egg	2 egg yolks, plus 1 tablespoon water
	2 egg yolks (in custard and such mixtures)
1 cup fresh sweet milk	$\frac{1}{2}$ cup evaporated milk plus $\frac{1}{2}$ cup water; powdered milk plus water; 1 cup sour milk or buttermilk plus $\frac{1}{2}$ teaspoon soda (or 2 teaspoons baking powder)
1 cup sour milk or buttermilk	1 tablespoon lemon juice or vinegar plus enough fresh sweet milk to make 1 cup
1 square unsweetened chocolate (1 oz)	3 tablespoons cocoa plus 1 ablespoon shortening
1 cup honey	$\frac{3}{4}$ cup sugar plus $\frac{1}{4}$ cup liquid
1 cup canned tomatoes	about $1\frac{1}{3}$ cups fresh tomatoes, simmered 10 minutes

E. Deep frying temperatures

Food		
Fish, small whole	370 F	3 to 5 minutes
Fish, fillets	370 F	4 to 6 minutes
Fish, oysters, clams	375 F	1 to 3 minutes
Croquettes, fish balls, or other precooked ingredients	360–400 F	2 minutes or until brown
Fritters, all raw ingredients	375 F	2 to 5 minutes

If you have no deep-frying thermometer, use this bread test.

For large pieces of raw food—335° to 360° F. A one-inch cube of bread from the soft part of the loaf will cook to golden brown in 1 to 1½ minutes.

For small pieces of raw food or large pieces of cooked food—340° to 380° F. Bread will brown in 50 to 60 seconds.

For most cooked foods—360° to 400° F. Bread will brown in 40 to 50 seconds.

USEFUL COOKING HINTS

The following odds and ends of information have been garnered over years of cooking experience. Though they do not all pertain exclusively to oriental cookery, they make good common sense and therefore ought to be part of the cook's general store of knowledge. I present them here in the hope that they will make cooking easier and more fun for you.

1. Measurements

As I have already pointed out, accurate measurement is important to satisfactory results from any recipe. In this book, and in most other cookbooks, measurements are given in terms of level, not heaping, teaspoons, tablespoons, and cups full. Always sift flour before measuring it. Brown sugar is usually packed before measuring. Do not shake the cup in measuring rice.

2. Orderliness

Read the recipe thoroughly until you are well acquainted with its nature and with the ingredients called for. Next assemble the ingredients and utensils. Then execute all of the preparatory steps. You will find that in many oriental foods, preparations are time-consuming. It is wise, therefore, to do as many of them as possible beforehand, since there is rarely time to stop during the cooking process.

3. Treating fruits and vegetables

Always wash vegetables and fruits—especially those intended for salads—in pure water. Wash all fresh vegetables before storing them in the refrigerator. Pare and cut vegetables and fruits immediately prior to use in order to prevent them from losing vitamin content. Canned fruits and vegetables, too, should be opened just before use for the same reason. Water in which vegetables have been cooked should be reserved for use in gravies and soups.

4. Miscellaneous ingredients
In cooking noodles, a tablespoon of butter or oil added to the water will prevent the noodles' sticking together.

Thaw frozen meats and fish slowly at room temperature. Unless meat is completely thawed before cooking it will be tough.

A pinch of salt added to egg whites will make them easier to whip.

5. Control of odors
A piece of bread placed on top of cabbage or cauliflower will absorb the odors these vegetables give off during cooking.

Orange or lemon rind will remove fishy odors from cooking water, utensils, or your hands.

Onion smells may be removed from cooking utensils in the following way. Fill the pan or pot with boiling water and a small quantity of wood ash—or soda—and allow it to stand for a short while on the back of the stove.

6. Care of utensils
Before scalding or boiling milk, rinse the pan with hot water to prevent the milk from coating the bottom.

Remove lime from tea kettles by boiling in them water to which a small amount of vinegar has been added.

Freshen coffee pots or teapots—other than silver ones—by filling them with cold water and wood ash, and gradually bringing the mixture to a boil.

Allow the kettle to cool, wash with soap and hot water, and rinse several times with boiling water.

China

The splendors of the Chinese cuisine rank it with the leading branches of culinary art of the world. In a sampling as limited as this, it would be impossible to do justice to the many regional delicacies and special cooking techniques employed in the various parts of China. For that reason I have selected a number of foods that are easily prepared and guaranteed to please all palates.

It is important to remember that the cooking in Chinese food rarely takes as much time as the preparation. Your work will go easier if you do all the cutting, trimming, marinating, and other preparatory steps before beginning to cook.

Sautéed foods are numerous in Chinese cooking. They are always prepared over a high heat with best-quality oil. The ingredients are cooked very briefly, and they must be stirred constantly. When they have reached just the right color and degree of tenderness, the seasonings and other ingredients are added, and the mixture is cooked for a few more minutes. The wok or traditional round-bottom frying pan, is very convenient for the preparation of Chinese sautéed foods.

Chinese braised foods are much like Western braised foods except for ingredients and should therefore cause very little difficulty. Steaming, on the other hand, is more widely used in China than in the West. Although the Chinese have special bamboo and wicker steamers, the Western cook will find the metal ones available in many oriental markets more practical and easier to keep clean. It is wise to add steaming to your cooking repertory because it produces delicate flavors and results in little loss of nutrition.

Beauty is an important part of Chinese, as it is of Japanese, food but the effects desired differ sharply. Whereas the Japanese prefer foods to retain their natural shapes, Chinese cooks are fonder of cutting foods into patterned pieces of uniform shape and of achieving striking effects by combining colors.

Ginger Chicken Hors d'oeuvre

(6 servings)

INGREDIENTS

boned cooked meat from $\frac{1}{2}$ frying chicken

2 cucumbers
2 tomatoes

SEASONINGS A

$\frac{1}{2}$ tsp grated ginger root
4 tbsp soy sauce
$2\frac{1}{2}$ tbsp vinegar
dash pepper
dash monosodium glutamate
2 tbsp sesame oil
2 tsp sugar

SEASONINGS B

$\frac{1}{2}$ tsp monosodium glutamate
1 tsp salt
1 tbsp sesame oil (if desired)

PREPARATION

1. Cool the chicken meat if it has been freshly cooked.
2. Combine seasonings A in a bowl and marinate the chicken in it for from 30 minutes to an hour.
3. Slice the tomatoes thin and cut the slices into semicircles.
4. Slice the cucumbers thin and marinate them in combined seasonings B till they are pliant.
5. Remove the chicken from the marinade and mound it in the center of a serving plate. Reserve the marinade.
6. Arrange the tomato and cucumber slices around the chicken and pour the reserved marinade over them. Many professional Chinese cooks cut the cucumbers into thin, fancy shapes for use as an ornamental garnish.

Cucumbers in Vinegar Dressing

(4 servings)

INGREDIENTS

6 medium cucumbers
3 shiso leaves (beefsteak plant; see p. 207)
1-inch section of fresh ginger root
1½ tbsp salt
2½ tbsp white vinegar or rice vinegar

1½ tbsp soy sauce
1½ tbsp sugar
½ tsp fresh ginger juice squeezed from grated, skinned fresh ginger root
1 tsp sesame oil
½ tsp monosodium glutamate

PREPARATION

1. Peel the cucumbers partially, leaving occasional ¼ inch strips of green peel to add color to the finished dish. Cut the cucumbers in half lengthwise, scoop out the seeds with a spoon, and slice the halves crosswise into thin slices.

2. Sprinkle the cucumbers with salt and let stand at least 15 minutes at room temperature. Then rinse cucumbers under cold water. Gently squeeze to reduce moisture. Place cucumbers in colander and refrigerate.

3. Rinse shiso leaves in cold water, pat dry with paper towels. Sprinkle lightly with salt, then rub, rinse, and squeeze out moisture. Slice in long, thin strips.

4. Scrap the outer skin from the ginger root. Cut it in julienne strips. Place the shredded shiso leaves and ginger root in the refrigerator.

5. Combine vinegar, soy sauce, sugar, ginger juice, sesame oil, and monosodium glutamate. Mix well.

6. In a salad bowl, combine cucumbers, shiso leaves, and ginger. Add dressing and toss to coat vegetables thoroughly.

Chicken Salad

(4 to 6 servings)

INGREDIENTS

1 3-lb whole chicken
1 bunch parsley leaves

1 tsp salt
4 tbsp plum sauce (see p. 203)

1 bunch green onion tops finely
 shredded in 1½-inch lengths
4 tbsp ketchup
½ tsp monosodium glutamate

1 tbsp parched sesame seeds
cellophane noodles (see p. 202)
vegetable oil
shredded lettuce garnish

PREPARATION

1. Wash chicken under cold water and pat dry inside and out with paper towels. Tie the wings with string and hang the chicken in a cool place for 2 hours to dry the skin.

2. Heat 2 cups oil in a large skillet over high heat. Turn heat down to moderate if oil begins to smoke. Fry chicken whole, half or quartered, depending upon size of skillet. When done, drain on paper towels. When cool, bone the chicken and tear the meat into fine, thin strips.

3. Deep fry the cellophane noodles until crisp, but not too brown. Drain and place on a platter over a bed of shredded lettuce.

4. Combine ketchup, monosodium glutamate, salt, plum sauce, sesame seeds, green onion, and shredded chicken. Toss until thoroughly mixed.

5. Place chicken mixture over cellophane noodles. Garnish with parsley.

Tea Eggs

INGREDIENT
1 dozen eggs
2 tsp black tea
1½ to 2 tbsp salt

1 tsp black pepper
1 star anise
⅓ cup soy sauce

PREPARATION

1. Place eggs in saucepan. Cover the eggs with water and boil for 30 minutes.

2. Soak in cold water and crack the shell all over with the back of a spoon. Return the eggs to the water in the saucepan without removing the shells.

3. Add the remaining ingredients to the saucepan and bring to a boil over high heat. Then reduce heat to a simmer, cover, and cook for 2 hours.

4. Turn off the heat and leave the eggs in the tea liquid at room

temperature for at least 8 hours.

5. When ready to serve, remove shells. The outer whites of the eggs should be marbled with dark lines resulting from the cracks in the shells. Cut the eggs in a decorative manner and serve. If the eggs are too salty, their taste can be moderated by soaking them in fresh water.

Asparagus with Crab Sauce

(4 servings)

INGREDIENTS

10 fresh asparagus spears
1 small can crab meat
$\frac{1}{2}$ tbsp cornstarch
1 tbsp water

$\frac{1}{2}$ cup milk
$\frac{3}{4}$ cup chicken stock
$\frac{1}{4}$ tsp monosodium glutamate
1 tsp salt

PREPARATION

1. Wash asparagus and cut off and discard hard ends.
2. Cook in boiling salted water till tender. Drain well.
3. Remove bone from crab meat. In skillet, over medium heat, bring chicken stock to a boil. Add crab meat and milk and simmer for 2 minutes. Mix cornstarch with water and add to the chicken stock, stirring occasionally until the sauce thickens. Reduce heat and add salt and monosodium glutamate to taste.
4. Put asparagus on a heated serving dish and pour crab-meat sauce over it.

Stir-fried Snow Peas with Mushrooms and Bamboo Shoots

(4 servings)

INGREDIENTS

$\frac{1}{2}$ cup blanched almonds
8 water chestnuts
4 dried mushrooms
1 lb fresh snow peas
4 small bamboo shoots
2 slices fresh ginger
1 clove garlic mashed

1 tbsp dry sherry
1 tbsp cornstarch
$\frac{1}{2}$ tsp sugar
$\frac{1}{2}$ tsp salt
1 tbsp soy sauce
$\frac{1}{4}$ tsp white pepper
3 tbsp vegetable oil

1. Soak mushrooms in water till soft. Reserve water. Discard stems and, after draining, cut caps into quarters.

2. Snap off and discard ends of snow peas and remove strings from them. Slice bamboo shoots and water chestnuts $\frac{1}{8}$ inch thick.

3. Heat 3 tbsp oil in skillet over high heat and add garlic. Reduce heat to moderate and sauté garlic till lightly browned. Add mushrooms, bamboo shoots, sugar, ginger, and dry sherry. Stir-fry for 3 minutes.

5. Add snow peas, salt, and pepper. Mix cornstarch with 2 tbsp water in which mushrooms were soaked. Add cornstarch to skillet and stir for a few seconds until the vegetables are coated with a light, transparent glaze. Add soy sauce and cook at high heat about 2 minutes, stirring constantly. Arrange in serving dish and sprinkle with almonds.

Stir-fried Bean Sprouts

(4 servings)

INGREDIENTS

2 lb bean sprouts
2 oz cooked ham shredded
2 green onions shredded
2 slices fresh ginger root shredded
3 tbsp peanut or salad oil

$\frac{1}{2}$ tsp salt
dash monosodium glutamate
2 tbsp soy sauce
1 tsp sesame oil

PREPARATION

1. Wash bean sprouts in large colander under cold running water. Drain and pat dry with paper towels.

2. Heat 3 tbsp peanut oil in a skillet, add salt, onion, ginger, and bean sprouts together. Stir-fry for 2 or 3 minutes over a high heat.

3. Add ham and monosodium glutamate, stirring quickly. Sprinkle mixture with soy sauce and sesame oil.

Fried Shrimp

(8 servings)

INGREDIENTS

2 lbs raw shrimp
5 tbsp hoisin sauce (see p. 199)
4 tbsp sugar
1 2-inch piece ginger root minced
3 cloves garlic mashed
2 tsp salt
1 tsp white pepper
4 tbsp white or rice vinegar

3 green onions cut into 1-inch
  lengths
2 tsp cornstarch
3 tbsp water
1 tsp soy sauce
4 tbsp oil
lemon slices

PREPARATION

1. Shell and devein shrimp and wash in cold water. Drain and pat dry with paper towels. Place shrimps in bowl and sprinkle with white pepper.

2. In a small bowl, mix hoisin sauce, sugar, 1 tsp salt, and vinegar.

3. Heat oil in skillet, add garlic. Fry shrimp 1 minute on each side. Sprinkle with 1 tsp salt and add ginger, green onion, and hoisin sauce mixture.

4. Briefly stir-fry then add cornstarch dissolved in mixture of water and soy sauce. Toss shrimp lightly to coat well.

5. Remove shrimp to a heated serving platter and cover with sauce. Garnish with lemon slices.

Shrimp and Vegetable Sauté

(4 servings)

INGREDIENTS

½ lb shelled small shrimp
2 small bamboo shoots
1 green pepper
1 carrot
1 dried shiitake mushroom

½ small onion
2 water chestnuts or 1 small potato
1 tbsp minced green onion
2 tbsp canned or cooked green
  peas

SEASONINGS A

½ tsp sake
1 tbsp cornstarch
1 egg white

dash salt
dash monosodium glutamate

SEASONINGS **B**

½ tsp salt
½ tsp sugar
1 tbsp sake
1 tsp monosodium glutamate

1 tbsp cornstarch dissolved in
  1 tbsp water
dash pepper

PREPARATION

1. After softening the shiitake mushroom in water, cut it, the carrot, bamboo shoots, green pepper, onion, and water chestnut in uniform small dice. Combine all vegetables except the onion.

2. Combine seasonings A and marinate the shrimp in the mixture.

3. In another bowl combine seasonings B.

4. Heat about ½ cup cooking oil in a heavy skillet or traditional Chinese frying pan, called a wok.

5. Remove the shrimp from the marinade and sauté them very briefly. As soon as they change color, remove and drain them.

6. Briefly sauté all the vegetables except the onion. They must not lose their color. Remove and drain.

7. Reduce oil in skillet to about 2 tbsp. In this sauté the onion till golden.

8. Add shrimp, sautéed vegetables, and seasonings B.

9. Over a high heat, sauté this mixture until the sauce thickens. Stir constantly during the cooking process. Serve at once.

Sautéed Liver with Pineapple

(4 servings)

INGREDIENTS

½ lb pork (or beef) liver sliced thin
1 small fresh pineapple peeled, cored, sliced and cut into fan-shape pieces (canned pineapple may be substituted)

1 cup thinly sliced mushrooms
½ green onion chopped
1 small piece ginger root sliced very thin
oil

SEASONINGS A

¼ tsp salt
dash pepper
dash monosodium glutamate

1 tbsp sake
1 tbsp cornstarch
1 tbsp oil

SEASONINGS B

1 tbsp soy sauce

1 tbsp vinegar

1 tbsp sugar

1 tbsp sake

½ tsp monosodium glutamate

3 tbsp stock

1 tbsp cornstarch dissolved in

  1 tbsp water

1 tsp sesame oil

PREPARATION

1. Combine seasonings A, adding cornstarch and oil last.

2. In a separate bowl combine seasonings B, except sesame oil.

3. Heat ½ cup oil in a heavy skillet. Sauté the liver slices till they change color. Remove and drain.

4. Lightly sauté the pineapple slices if they are fresh. This is not necessary if canned pineapple is used.

5. Discard oil in which liver was fried and heat 2 tbsp fresh oil in a skillet. In this sauté the green onion and ginger slices.

6. Add all other ingredients, except seasonings B, and sauté briefly.

7. Add seasonings B to the pan and, stirring constantly, cook until the sauce thickens.

8. The reserved ½ tsp of sesame oil is poured over the mixture immediately before serving.

Pork and Cashew Nuts

(4 servings)

INGREDIENTS

about 1 cup diced raw pork

½ cup cashew nuts (unsalted)

1 tbsp fresh ginger root cut
  in very thin slices

2 green onions cut into 1-inch
  lengths

15 peppercorns

3 (or less) chopped chili peppers

SEASONINGS A

¼ tsp salt

½ tsp soy sauce

1 tbsp sake

¼ tsp monosodium glutamate

1 lightly beaten egg white

1½ tbsp cornstarch

1 tbsp oil

1½ tbsp soy sauce
1 tbsp vinegar
1 tbsp sugar
1 tbsp sake
dash monosodium glutamate

1 tbsp cornstarch dissolved
  in 1 tbsp water
2 tbsp stock or water
1 tbsp oil

PREPARATION

1. Combine seasonings A and marinate the diced pork in the mixture for 30 minutes.

2. In a skillet heat 2 tbsp oil and sauté the cashew nuts briefly. Remove and drain.

3. In a separate bowl combine seasonings B.

4. In a heavy skillet heat about 5 tbsp cooking oil. In this sauté the peppercorns and chili till the chili turns black.

5. Remove peppercorns and chili; discard.

6. Remove the pork from the marinade and sauté it in the peppery oil till it changes color.

7. Add green onion, ginger slices, cashews and seasonings B. Stirring constantly, cook till the sauce thickens.

Cabbage Rolls Stuffed with Pork

(4 servings)

INGREDIENTS

4 large cabbage leaves parboiled
¼ lb ground pork

1 lightly beaten egg
cornstarch for dredging

SEASONINGS A
dash salt
dash pepper

dash monosodium glutamate
1 tbsp cornstarch

SEASONINGS B
1 tbsp oyster sauce or
  Worcestershire sauce
1 tbsp oil
1½ tbsp soy sauce
1½ tsp sugar

½ cup stock
1 tbsp cornstarch dissolved
  in 1 tbsp water
dash pepper
additional soy sauce as needed

PREPARATION

1. Combine and mix well pork, egg, and seasonings A.

2. After trimming the hard lower sections from the parboiled cabbage leaves, dredge them in cornstarch.

3. Dividing the meat stuffing into four equal parts, place one part on each cabbage leaf. Folding the outer edges inward, roll the cabbage leaves securely to enclose the stuffing.

4. Bring water to a boil in the lower section of a steamer.

5. Place the cabbage rolls, seams down, on an oiled heat-proof dish. Put the dish in the upper section of the steamer, cover, and steam for from 15 to 20 minutes.

6. Remove and cut into bite-size pieces. Keep warm.

7. Prepare sauce by combining seasonings B in a saucepan and cooking over moderate heat till the mixture thickens. Pour the sauce over the cabbage rolls and serve at once.

Beef and Onion Sauté

(4 servings)

INGREDIENTS
about ¾ cup lean beef cut in julienne strips
2 small onions sliced

SEASONINGS A
¼ tsp salt
1 tbsp sake
dash pepper
½ tsp baking powder

¼ tsp monosodium glutamate
1 egg lightly beaten
1½ tbsp cornstarch
1 tbsp oil

SEASONINGS B
1½ tbsp soy sauce
1 tbsp sake
1 tsp sugar
⅔ tsp monosodium glutamate

1 tbsp cornstarch dissolved
    in 1 tbsp water
3 tbsp stock or water

PREPARATION

1. After combining all seasonings A, except the oil and cornstarch, in a bowl, add the beef slices and mix well. Add the cornstarch; mix well. Finally add the oil and mix again.

2. Combine seasonings B in a separate bowl.

3. Heat ½ cup oil in a heavy skillet. Sauté the onions lightly. Add the beef and sauté till it changes color.

4. Pour combined seasonings B over the onions and beef and, stirring constantly, cook until the sauce thickens. Serve at once.

Rice-coated Meatballs

(4 servings)

INGREDIENTS

½ cup glutinous rice
1 lb ground lean pork
4 dried shiitake mushrooms
1 egg beaten
1 can water chestnuts minced
1 small bamboo shoot minced
2 slices fresh ginger root minced
1 green onion minced
1 tsp sugar

1 tbsp dry sherry
1 tsp salt
¼ tsp white pepper
1 tbsp soy sauce
½ tsp monosodium glutamate
1 tbsp cornstarch
1 bunch parsley
1 large tomato
1 tbsp tomato ketchup

PREPARATION

1. Wash rice in a colander under cold running water until the water runs clear. Drain thoroughly. In a small bowl, cover the rice with 1 cup of cold water and soak covered for 8 hours or overnight in the refrigerator.

2. Drain the rice on a cloth towel spread over a colander.

3. In a small bowl, cover the mushrooms with ½ cup of water. Sprinkle them with 1 tsp sugar. Soak for 30 minutes. Drain. Discard mushroom stems and mince the caps.

4. Combine ground pork, egg, water chestnuts, bamboo shoots, ginger, green onion, dry sherry, white pepper, soy sauce, monosodium glutamate, salt, and cornstarch. Mix well with your fingers until the ingredients are thoroughly blended.

5. Coat your hands with cornstarch and make about 20 small meatballs 1 inch in diameter.

6. Roll the meatballs gently in soaked and drained glutinous rice, pressing them to coat each meatball well.

7. Place meatballs on steamer rack. Set them well apart on a moistened double thickness of cheesecloth or a clean cloth napkin to prevent

the balls from sticking together. Bring the water in the steamer to a boil and cover first with a clean cloth napkin then with the lid. Steam the rice-coated meatballs for 30 minutes.

8. Arrange on a serving dish with parsley. Make a ketchup container by slashing a tomatoe in 8 places (not through the base). Fill the tomatoe with ketchup and place it in the center of the serving dish. Arrange the meat balls around the tomato. Serve at once. (You may add food coloring (pink or green) to the water in which the glutinous rice is soaked.)

Stuffed Fish

(4 to 6 servings)

INGREDIENTS

1 scaled and cleaned 3-lb whole red snapper, bass, cod, haddock, bluefish, or whitefish

STUFFING

4 Chinese dried shrimps	¼ tsp pepper
6 water chestnuts	1 tsp sugar
4 dried shiitake mushrooms	1 tbsp soy sauce
1 slice smoked ham	2 tsp cornstarch
3 green onions thinly sliced	3 tbsp water
2 tbsp chopped parsley	1 tbsp oil
½ tsp salt	cornstarch for dredging

SAUCE

1 slice ginger root minced	½ cup chicken stock
2 tbsp dry sherry	1 tsp cornstarch
1 tbsp sugar	¼ tsp monosodium glutamate
1 tbsp soy sauce	

PREPARATION

1. Wash fish well under cold running water. Drain well; pat dry with paper towels. Sprinkle fish inside and out with salt and cornstarch; rub well into skin. With sharp knife, make deep cuts about 2 inches apart along both sides of fish.

2. In a small bowl, soak shrimps and mushrooms until soft, then mince. Mince water chestnuts and ham. Mix these ingredients and add

chopped parsley, green onions, $\frac{1}{2}$ tsp salt, pepper, sugar, soy sauce, oil, and cornstarch blended with water. Mix well.

3. Stuff fish with this mixture and close opening with skewers or toothpicks.

4. Heat about $\frac{1}{8}$ inch of oil in large size skillet and brown fish on both sides.

5. Mix all sauce ingredients in a bowl and pour over fish. Cover and braise fish for 2 minutes. Turn fish over, re-cover skillet, and continue braising 10 to 15 minutes. Remove fish to heated serving platter.

Steamed Fish

INGREDIENTS

1 whole fresh sole, red snapper, cod, haddock, bluefish, or white fish cleaned but with head intact

SEASONINGS

1 tsp salt	2 dried shiitake mushrooms
$\frac{1}{2}$ tsp pepper	1 thin slice smoked ham
2 tbsp dry sherry	2 dried oriental red dates
$\frac{1}{2}$ tsp sugar	3 slices fresh ginger root
2 tbsp cornstarch	1 green onion
2 tbsp soy sauce	1 dozen dried lily flowers
2 tbsp oil	3 sprigs parsley

PREPARATION

1. Clean and wash fish well in cold running water. Pat dry with paper towels. Sprinkle fish inside and outside with salt. Mix the seasonings and rub half the mixture into fish. Place in large serving dish and set aside.

2. Soak mushrooms, dried lily flowers, and oriental red dates until soft. Slice dates and mushrooms thin. Cut dried lily flowers in half. Julienne slice ham and ginger. Chop green onion. Spread remaining seasonings over surface of fish.

3. Bring water in the lower part of a steamer to a boil over a high heat. Place fish and serving dish on the steamer rack. Lay a cloth or dish towel over the top of the steamer before putting the lid on. This prevents condensed water from dripping on the fish. Cover the steamer tightly and steam for about 20 minutes. (If you do not have a steamer, use a large pan with a tightly fitting lid. Place 3 small, ovenproof bowls

in the bottom. Put a rack on top of the bowls and fill the pan with water to 1 inch above the rack). Sprinkle the steamed fish with additional chopped parsley before serving.

Carp Braised in Chicken Fat

INGREDIENTS

1 3-lb carp cleaned and scaled
¼ cup chicken fat
1 or 2 cakes bean curd cut
   in 1-inch cubes
1 small ginger root sliced thin
1 clove garlic mashed
parsley, lemon

1 green onion cut in 2-inch
   lengths
1 tsp salt
1 tbsp Tabasco sauce
1 tbsp oyster sauce (see p. 202)
2 cups chicken broth
1 tbsp sugar

PREPARATION

1. Wash fish well under cold running water; drain well. Sprinkle inside and outside with salt.

2. Heat chicken fat in skillet large enough to hold the fish. Add garlic, ginger, Tabasco sauce, oyster sauce, green onion, and sugar. Bring to a boil.

3. Brown fish on both sides in hot chicken fat. Pour boiling chicken broth over the fish. Cover skillet and simmer for from 10 to 15 minutes or until fish is done. Remove fish to large heated serving platter.

4. Add bean curd to mixture in skillet and cook 5 minutes. Arrange bean curd around fish and pour sauce over both. Garnish platter with parsley and lemon wedges.

Paper-wrapped Prawns

(4 servings)

INGREDIENTS

4 prawns
8 slices peeled fresh ginger root
8 fresh or frozen snow peas
2 green onions cut in 2-inch
   lengths
1 tsp dry sherry
dash of salt
dash of white pepper

dash of monosodium glutamate
oil for frying
8 sheets of cellophane paper
   6 by 6 inches
1 tbsp melted butter
2 sprigs parsley
lemon wedges

1. Shell and devein prawns. Wash under cold running water and pat dry with paper towels.

2. Cut each prawn in half and place in small bowl. Sprinkle with sherry, salt, pepper, and monosodium glutamate. Mix well.

3. Brush each piece of cellophane paper with 1 tbsp melted butter. Place a slice of prawn, a slice of ginger, a slice of green onion, and one snow pea on the paper, then wrap securely.

4. Heat 2 cups oil. Deep fry prawn packages, seam side down, until prawns turn white. Garnish with lemon wedges and parsley.

Paper-wrapped Chicken

(4 servings)

INGREDIENTS

3–4 lb chicken
$\frac{1}{4}$ lb sliced smoked ham
2-inch section of fresh ginger
   root coarsely grated
1 green onion minced
1 tbsp dry sherry
2 tbsp soy sauce
$\frac{1}{2}$ tsp sugar
1 tbsp salad oil

1 tsp cornstarch
$\frac{1}{4}$ tsp salt
$\frac{1}{4}$ tsp pepper
dash monosodium glutamate
20 sheets of cellophane paper—
   4 by 4 inches
1 bunch of parsley or watercress
oil for frying

PREPARATION

1. Remove bones and skin from chicken. Cut white and dark meat into pieces about $\frac{1}{8}$ inch thick, $\frac{1}{2}$ inch wide, and $1\frac{1}{2}$ inches long. Cut slices of ham into 20 thin pieces.

2. Place the chicken in a bowl. Combine dry sherry, soy sauce, sugar, oil, cornstarch, salt, pepper, and monosodium glutamate. Add chopped green onion and grated ginger. Marinate chicken in this mixture for 10 minutes.

3. Divide the chicken and ham into 20 equal portions. Place chicken on square of cellophane paper, top with a slice of ham, then wrap it securely to form a small package.

4. Heat about 1 inch of oil in a skillet. Fry the packages for about

2 minutes on each side until light brown in color. Drain the packages and place on a serving plate. Garnish with parsley or watercress.

Pork-ball Casserole

(4 servings)

INGREDIENTS

1 lb finely chopped or ground
  pork
1 egg
1 bunch Chinese chard
  (see p. 197)
3 green onions

1 2-inch section fresh ginger root
10 shrimp
1 cake bean curd
1 mushroom
2 small bamboo shoots
2 tbsp cornstarch

SEASONINGS A

1 tbsp soy sauce
1 tbsp sake
1 tsp sugar

$\frac{1}{2}$ tsp salt
dash pepper
dash monosodium glutamate

SEASONINGS B

1 tsp salt
1 tsp sake

dash monosodium glutamate

PREPARATION

1. Chop enough of one green onion to make 1 tbsp. Combine the chopped onion with the pork, beaten egg, cornstarch, and seasonings A to which have been added 2 tsp ginger juice crushed from one of the pieces of ginger root. Chop the mushroom and the bamboo shoots. Add to the meat mixture. Mix thoroughly and shape into 12 small balls.

2. Bring water to a boil in the bottom section of a steamer. Steam meatballs for 15 minutes. Reserve juices.

3. Wash Chinese chard thoroughly and slice in half lengthwise. Parboil it. Shell and devein shrimp. Wash in salted water and drain.

4. Cut the bean curd cake into 16 cubes. Slice the remaining green onions into 1-inch digonal sections. Peel and thinly slice the remaining section of ginger root. Cut Chinese chard into 3-inch lengths.

5. Into a heated shabu-shabu pan (see next page), put the prepared

ingredients, the juices reserved from steaming the meat balls, and seasonings B. Simmer briefly before serving.

Asparagus and Beef

(4 servings)

INGREDIENTS

2 lb sirloin, round roast, or
  prime roast
1 bunch fresh asparagus
1 clove garlic chopped
½ small piece grated ginger
1 tbsp sugar
1 tbsp sake
½ tsp salt

1 tbsp rice vinegar
½ tbsp sesame oil
1 tbsp cornstarch
dash pepper
dash monosodium glutamate
4 tbsp salad oil
1 tbsp soy sauce

PREPARATION

1. Slice meat into very thin 1½-inch lengths. Mix with sugar, sake (or sherry), vinegar, sesame oil, cornstarch, monosodium glutamate, and pepper. Let stand for 1 hour.

2. Wash asparagus and break each stalk at lowest point at which it will snap easily. With a knife remove scales, then rinse stalks under running water. Cut each asparagus stalk into 2½-inch lengths.

3. Add garlic to grated ginger.

4. Heat skillet and add 2 tbsp salad oil. Use a high heat. When oil is very hot, add asparagus, salt, monosodium glutamate, and pepper. Sauté until asparagus is tender (about 6–10 minutes). Remove to a large platter and keep warm.

5. Pour 2 tbsp oil into skillet. Brown garlic and ginger. Add beef and stir-sauté about 5 minutes. Add soy sauce. Cook beef until almost done. Place meat in center of asparagus. Serve immediately. The following sauce is a tasty addition to this dish.

SAUCE INGREDIENTS

2 tbsp chicken stock or broth	1 tbsp water
1 tbsp oyster sauce	½ tsp soy sauce
1 tsp cornstarch	monosodium glutamate

Combine ingredients and heat till clear and thick.

Beef and Spinach

(4 servings)

INGREDIENTS

1 lb sirloin or round roast	1 tsp cornstarch
1 bunch fresh spinach	2 tsp soy sauce
1 clove garlic	dash pepper
2 tsp sugar	pinch monosodium glutamate
2 tsp sake	3 tbsp salad oil
2 tsp vinegar	1 tsp cornstarch
2 tsp sesame oil	½ small ginger root
⅓ tsp salt	

PREPARATION

1. Cut meat in very thin, 1-inch long strips. Mix with sugar, sake, vinegar, sesame-oil, cornstarch, monosodium glutamate and a dash of pepper. Let marinate for a few minutes.

2. Remove stems from spinach, cut in pieces 1½ inches long, and soak in cool water; drain.

3. Chop garlic and ginger.

4. Heat skillet then add 1 tbsp salad oil. Add spinach, $\frac{1}{3}$ tsp salt, and dash each of pepper and monosodium glutamate. Sauté briefly. Remove from skillet.

5. Add 2 tbsp more oil. Brown garlic and ginger. Put beef in skillet. Add soy sauce and sauté till beef is nearly done. Add spinach. Thicken with cornstarch dissolved in water. Oyster sauce may be added if desired.

Barbecued Pork

INGREDIENTS

5 lb boneless pork, preferably butt
4 green onions minced
1 tsp ginger root grated
$\frac{1}{4}$ cup dry sherry
4 tbsp sugar
2 tbsp Chinese brown bean sauce (see soy sauce, p. 206)
1 tsp sesame seeds
1 tsp salt

1 tbsp hoisin sauce (see p. 199)
3 tbsp plum sauce (see p. 203)
1 tsp cinnamon
$\frac{1}{2}$ tsp molasses or honey
3 tsp salt
1 tsp sesame oil
2 to 3 drops red food coloring
dash of garlic powder
$\frac{1}{4}$ tsp monosodium glutamate

PREPARATION

1. Cut the pork butt into strips 6 by 2 inches. Lay the strips flat in a large baking pan.

2. Combine ground ginger, bean sauce, sherry, sugar, hoisin sauce, plum sauce, cinnamon, molasses, salt, sesame oil, green onion, dash of garlic powder, and 2 or 3 drops red food coloring. Stir until the ingredients are well mixed. In this marinade mixture arrange pork strips in one layer. Turn them over and spoon the marinade over them. Let marinate for at least 6 hours in the refrigerator. Turn the pork strips from time to time.

3. Preheat the oven to 250°. Place the racks in highest position in oven. Line the oven floor with aluminum foil to catch drippings from the pork. Hang the pork strips from the rack with paper clips or hooks. Roast the pork undisturbed for 10 minutes. Then increase heat to 350° and roast for another 10 minutes. Increase the heat to 450° and

roast for 15 minutes. Remove the pork strips; baste with marinade then continue roasting for 1 hour and 15 minutes or until they are crisp and rich, golden brown.

4. Remove the pork from the oven, take out the hooks, and cut the strips diagonally into slices $\frac{1}{8}$ inch thick. Arrange in overlapping layers on a heated platter. Serve with lightly parched sesame seeds and 1 tsp of salt and $\frac{1}{4}$ tsp monosodium glutamate mixed in a small bowl.

Lamb Szechwan

(4 servings)

INGREDIENTS

$\frac{1}{2}$ lb thinly sliced, lean lamb

2 stalks celery

$\frac{1}{2}$ cup snow peas

$\frac{1}{2}$ cup sliced mushrooms

2 tbsp minced green onion.

1 tbsp grated fresh ginger root

1 clove garlic mashed

few drops Tabasco sauce

SEASONINGS A

1 tsp salt

1 tbsp sake

1 tbsp oil

dash monosodium glutamate

1 egg lightly beaten

1 tbsp cornstarch

SEASONINGS B

2 tbsp soy sauce

1 tsp vinegar

1 heaping tsp sugar

2 tbsp cornstarch dissolved
  in 2 tbsp water

2 tbsp stock or water

PREPARATION

1. Combine and mix seasonings A in a bowl. Marinate the lamb slices in the mixture for about 30 minutes.

2. After cleaning and scraping it, cut the celery into diamond-shaped pieces. Clean and string the snow peas.

3. Heat $\frac{1}{2}$ cup oil in a heavy skillet. Sauté the lamb slices till they change color. Remove and drain.

4. Briefly sauté the celery and snow peas. Remove and drain.

5. Reduce the oil in the pan to about 2 tbsp; add a few drops of Tabasco sauce. Over a high heat, briefly sauté the lamb once again.

6. Add the remaining ingredients. Stirring constantly, add the seasonings B. Cook until the sauce thickens. Serve at once.

Steamed Chicken Mound

(4 servings)

INGREDIENTS

3 lightly beaten egg whites
½ cup boned, diced chicken
   breast meat
¼ cup thinly sliced mushrooms

3 tbsp condensed milk
1 tbsp lard or other unseasoned
   shortening
cooked green peas for garnish

SEASONINGS A
dash salt
dash monosodium glutamate

½ tsp sake

SEASONINGS B
dash salt
dash monosodium glutamate

½ tsp sake

SEASONINGS C
1 cup stock
dash salt
dash sugar

1 tsp sesame oil
1 tbsp parched sesame seeds.

PREPARATION

1. Sprinkle chicken meat with seasonings A and allow to stand for a few minutes.

2. Combine chicken with egg whites, condensed milk, seasonings B, and a little water if the mixture is very stiff. Mix well.

3. Grease the inside of a heatproof bowl large enough to hold the chicken mixture but of a size suited to your steamer.

4. Bring water to a boil in the bottom of the steamer. Put the bowl containing the chicken mixture into the top section, cover, and steam for about 20 minutes. Invert the bowl on a serving dish and remove the bowl carefully from the chicken mound.

5. Combine seasonings C, except the sesame oil and seeds, in a saucepan. Add the sliced mushrooms and cook until they are thoroughly heated. Add the sesame oil.

6. Pour this sauce over the chicken mound and sprinkle the parched sesame seeds and cooked green peas on top.

Baked Stuffed Green Peppers

(6 servings)

INGREDIENTS
6 green peppers seeded and cut in half
½ lb ground pork
3 water chestnuts pounded to a pulp or ½ cup cold mashed potatoes
parched white sesame seeds for garnish
cornstarch for dredging

SEASONINGS A
dash salt
dash pepper
dash monosodium glutamate

1 tsp sake
1 tsp cornstarch

SEASONINGS B
2 tsp soy sauce
2 tbsp vinegar
1 tbsp sake

2 heaping tsp sugar
1 tbsp cornstarch dissolved
    in 1 tbsp water
1 tbsp stock or water

PREPARATION
1. Preheat the oven to 300 degrees. After trimming the bottom of each pepper case to make it rest level in the pan, dust the insides with cornstarch.
2. Mix the pounded water chestnuts well with the pork and seasonings A.
3. Fill the pepper cases with the meat mixture and sprinkle the tops with sesame seed.
4. Bake for about 10 minutes.
5. Prepare the sauce by combining seasonings B in a saucepan and cooking until the mixture thickens.
6. When the peppers are done, cover them with the sauce.

Bitter Melon Stuffed with Meat

(4 servings)

INGREDIENTS

4 medium bitter melons
  (see p. 196)
½ lb lean pork ground fine
1 egg beaten
5 water chestnuts minced
1 small bamboo shoot minced
2 slices fresh ginger root minced
2 cloves garlic mashed
2 green onions minced
½ bunch parsley minced
1½ tbsp soy sauce
½ tsp sugar

4 tsp dry sherry
2 tsp cornstarch
½ tsp salt
¼ tsp white pepper
¼ tsp monosodium glutamate
2 tbsp vegetable or peanut oil
1 tbsp black bean sauce
  (see soy sauce, p. 206)
½ cup chicken stock
1 bunch watercress
green onion for garnish

PREPARATION

1. Cut bitter melon into disks 1½ inches thick. Scoop out white inner pulp.

2. Mix pork with water chestnuts, bamboo shoot, ginger, 1 clove garlic, green onion, beaten egg, and parsley.

3. Add 1 tbsp soy sauce, sugar, 3 tbsp sherry, and ¼ tsp monosodium glutamate. Mix well.

4. Stuff disks with meat mixture until filling bulges out on both sides. Sprinkle the stuffing in each slice with 1 tsp cornstarch.

5. Heat oil in skillet over high heat for 30 seconds. Reduce the heat to moderate if the oil begins to smoke. Fry stuffed disks on both sides until golden brown.

6. Add sauce made of 1 clove garlic crushed with blackbean sauce and diluted with chicken stock, remaining ½ tbsp soy sauce, 1 tsp dry sherry, ½ tsp salt, ¼ tsp pepper, and ¼ tsp monosodium glutamate. Cover and cook over low heat for 15 to 20 minutes. Thicken with 1 tsp cornstarch mixed with 2 tbsp water.

7. Place in warm serving dish and garnish with watercress and onion flowers made in the following way. Cut white part of a green onion into 2-inch lengths. Make several vertical incisions to half the length of the sections. Drop these into ice water. The cut ends will open into flower shapes.

Stuffed Mushrooms

(4 servings)

INGREDIENTS

8 large fresh mushrooms
½ lb minced pork
½ lb unshelled raw shrimp
1 bamboo shoot chopped fine
3 water chestnuts chopped fine
1 green onion
1 clove garlic mashed

2 tsp dry sherry
3 tbsp soy sauce
1 tbsp cornstarch
2 tbsp chicken stock
¼ tsp salt
½ tsp monosodium glutamate
5 sprigs parsley

PREPARATION

1. Clean mushrooms; remove and discard stems. Rinse, shell, and devein shrimp. Mince green onion and shrimp together. Mash ½ clove garlic.

2. Combine pork, shrimp, bamboo shoots, water chestnuts, green onion, and garlic.

3. Add remaining ingredients, except mushrooms and parsley. Mix thoroughly.

4. Fill mushroom caps with meat mixture. After filling, put between heatproof plates and steam in a tightly covered steamer 30 minutes.

5. Garnish with parsley.

Sweet-and-sour Pork

(4 servings)

INGREDIENTS

1 lb pork butt roast
1 carrot
1 green pepper
1 small onion
1 can bamboo shoots
2 slices pineapple
1 small piece ginger grated
1 clove garlic
2 dried shiitake mushrooms
soaked in ¾ cup water
1½ tbsp water

dash monosodium glutamate
6 tbsp sugar
1 tsp salt
3 tbsp soy sauce
1 tbsp vinegar with 3 tbsp
pineapple juice or 3 tbsp
rice vinegar
1 tbsp ketchup
½ tbsp sake
1 tbsp mirin (see p. 201)
cornstarch

1. Cut pork into 1 inch cubes. Marinate pork in mixture of 1 tbsp soy sauce, ½ tbsp sake, and grated ginger for 15 minutes. Coat marinated pork with cornstarch and deep fry in salad oil. For best results deep fry the pork twice, draining between fryings.

2. Slice bamboo shoots and onion. Cut green pepper into eighths and pineapple into six pieces. Reserve water in which they were soaked and slice shiitake mushrooms. Scrape carrot, slice, and cut into flower patterns. Boil until tender and plunge immediately into cold water to arrest cooking.

3. Mix water from mushrooms with sugar, salt, ketchup, monosodium glutamate, and 2 tbsp soy sauce.

4. Crush garlic and cook in 3 tbsp salad oil. Add vegetables in the following order: onion, mushrooms, bamboo shoots, green pepper, and carrot. Sauté the mixture.

5. To vegetables add mixture in item 3. Mix 1½ tbsp cornstarch with 1½ tbsp water. Add 1 tbsp vinegar with 3 tbsp pineapple juice. Combine this mixture with vegetables. Then add meat and pineapple. Add 1 tbsp mirin when done.

Sweet-and-sour Fish

(6 servings)

INGREDIENTS

1 scaled and cleaned white-flesh fish (about 3 lb)
½ lb lean pork cut julienne style
3 julienne cut dried shiitake mushrooms
1 julienne cut bamboo shoot
cornstarch
1 tsp salt

1 julienne cut carrot
½ onion thinly sliced
1 minced chili pepper
1 tbsp parsley chopped
2 tbsp soy sauce
¼ tsp grated ginger

SWEET-AND-SOUR SAUCE

3 tbsp cornstarch
⅓ cup sugar
⅓ cup vinegar

1 cup water
⅓ cup soy sauce
3 tbsp dry sherry or sake

1. Make 3 or 4 parallel, diagonal slashes about ½ inch deep in the upper and under sides of the fish. The head must remain intact on the fish, and the tail and fins must be trimmed, but not removed. Dry the fish well on paper towels. Srinkle fish inside and outside with a mixture of cornstarch and salt.

2. Mix 2 tbsp soy sauce and grated ginger in a small bowl and marinate the pork strips in this for 15 minutes.

3. Combine sauce ingredients in a small bowl.

4. Heat about 1 inch of cooking oil in a skillet large enough to accommodate the fish. Use high heat. Then lower to medium heat and fry fish for 2 minutes on each side. Repeat this process frying fish 4 minutes on each side. Remove carefully, drain on paper towels, and keep warm.

5. In a heavy skillet heat to the point of fragrance 2 tbsp cooking oil. Reduce heat to medium and sauté mushrooms briefly. Increase heat, add chili pepper, carrot, bamboo shoot, onion, and pork. Sauté till the pork is done. Add the sweet-and-sour sauce ingredients, reduce the heat, and cook till the sauce thickens.

6. Place the fried fish in the center of a large heated serving platter. Pour some of the sauce over the fish and arrange the pork and vegetable mixture around it. Sprinkle the fish with chopped parsley.

Sweet-and-sour Fish Cubes

(4 servings)

INGREDIENTS

¾ lb fillet of bass
1 tbsp dry sherry or sake
1 egg well beaten
8 dried shiitake mushrooms
1 medium sized onion sliced
1 green pepper cut in ½-inch slices
3 slices pineapple cut into eighths
1 zucchini cut in thin slices
1 diced carrot parboiled
1 piece fresh ginger root
1 tbsp soy sauce

4 tbsp cornstarch
4 tsp sugar
1 small clove garlic minced
salt
oil for deep frying

SWEET-AND-SOUR SAUCE

½ cup white vinegar
⅓ cup sugar
2 tbsp cornstarch
2 tbsp pineapple juice
2 tbsp ketchup
1 tsp soy sauce
1 tbsp hoisin sauce (see p. 199)

1. Rinse fish in cold water and pat dry with paper towels. Sprinkle inside and outside with salt.

2. Cut fish into 1-inch cubes and sprinkle with sherry or sake. Mix soy sauce with egg. Marinate in this mixture for 10 minutes. Remove fish from marinade and coat thoroughly with cornstarch.

3. Heat a wok or skillet over high heat for about 30 seconds. Add 2 cups oil. Fry fish for 3 to 5 minutes or until crisp. Drain on paper towels. Discard oil in which fish was fried.

4. Sauté minced garlic, vegetables, and pineapple in 1 tbsp hot oil. Add 1 tsp salt and 4 tsp sugar to vegetables. Mix thoroughly.

5. Add fish and heat quickly.

6. Mix sweet-and-sour sauce ingredients. Add it to fish, pineapple, and vegetables, stirring constantly until sauce is thick and fish is coated.

Rich Omelets

(4 servings)

INGREDIENTS

½ lb shredded pork, crab, shrimp, chicken, or barbecued pork

6–8 eggs beaten

¼ lb bean sprouts

6 green onions cut in 1-inch julienne strips

¼ cup smoked ham sliced in thin 1½-inch julienne strips

2 dried shiitake mushrooms

1 stalk celery sliced in thin 1½-inch julienne strips

1 small piece of ginger root minced

1½–2 tbsp soy sauce

½–1 tsp pepper

1 tsp sugar

1 tbsp cornstarch

oil

dash of monosodium glutamate

PREPARATION

1. Soak mushrooms in water for about 30 minutes or until soft. Remove and discard stems; slice caps.

2. Wash the bean sprouts in a colander under running cold water and drain; pat dry with paper towels.

3. Heat 1 tbsp oil in a skillet over high heat. Add ginger and shredded pork, and stir-fry for 1 minute. Then add celery, green onion,

mushrooms, ham, bean sprouts, salt, pepper, sugar, monosodium glutamate, and soy sauce. Stir-fry 1 minute then remove from skillet and
set aside. Reserve juices in skillet.

4. Stir beaten eggs into cooked ingredients. In a different skillet
heat 2 more tbsp oil. Lower heat to medium and pour in enough egg
mixture to form a small omelet. Fry on both sides until golden brown.
Repeat with the rest of mixture, making 4 omelets in all.

5. Heat the juice from the meat and vegetables. Mix 1 tbsp cornstarch
with 2 tbsp water and pour into the heated juices. Cook till thick
and clear. Pour gravy over omelets.

Mongolian Barbecue

(4 or 5 servings)

INGREDIENTS

a total of 1½ lbs of a mixture of thin sliced mutton, beef, pork, or
   venison.

2 oz suet	2 quartered green peppers
2 green onions cut into 2-inch lengths	8 mushrooms with stems removed
2 onions sliced thin	½ bunch edible chrysanthemum
½ head cabbage shredded	leaves in uniform sprigs

SAUCE A

juice of 1 lemon	1 tbsp grated ginger root
1 apple grated or ½ cup apple juice	2 tbsp mirin (see p. 201)
2 tbsp chopped green onions	5 tbsp soy sauce
2 cloves garlic mashed	5 tbsp sake or dry sherry
	dash monosodium glutamate

SAUCE B

5 tbsp soy sauce	5 tbsp sake or dry sherry
2 tbsp sesame oil	dash monosodium glutamate
dash Tabasco sauce	

CONDIMENTS

2 green onions cut julienne style, washed in cold water, and drained.
grated peel of 1 lemon with dash of garlic salt or 1 mashed garlic
   clove.

PREPARATION

1. Wash and prepare all vegetables and combine them attractively with the meat on a large serving platter.

2. Make the two sauces by combining the ingredients. Pour them into individual bowls, two for each guest.

3. Prepare the condiments and place them in serving dishes.

4. For this meal a special utensil (see above) is necessary. It has a domed iron section in the center. Heat it at the table. Place the suet on the center and allow the melted fat to run down, coating the dome evenly. Arrange the meat and vegetables over the dome. They may be eaten as soon as the meat changes color and the vegetables are tender. Guests may select the morsels they want and dip them in one of the two prepared sauces to which have been added either or both or the condiments.

Chicken Pot Roast

(6 servings)

INGREDIENTS

1 roasting chicken (3½ lb)	½ cup sugar
1 piece ginger root sliced	¼ cup sake
2 pieces stick cinnamon	2 tbsp sesame oil
1 cup soy sauce	½ cup water

PREPARATION

1. Combine soy sauce, sugar, water, and sake.

2. Heat skillet. Add 2 tbsp sesame oil, ginger, and 2 pieces stick cinnamon. Then add seasonings mixture (step 1) and heat. Add

chicken; baste several times with sauce. Bring to a boil. Reduce heat, simmer, covered, for from 40 to 50 minutes, until skin is golden and meat is done.

3. Cut into small pieces, cutting through bone, and serve.

Cantonese-style Roast Chicken

(4 servings)

INGREDIENTS

1 roasting chicken (3½ lb)
1 tbsp salt
¼ tsp cinnamon
¼ tbsp black pepper
1 tbsp molasses

2 tbsp boiling water
4 tbsp boiling water
1 tbsp peanut oil
3 tbsp sake or sherry

PREPARATION

1. Immerse the chicken in boiling water for 2 minutes. Remove and drain. Combine salt, cinnamon, and black pepper. Roast mixed seasonings in 350 F oven 5 minutes.

2. Rub roasted salt mixture inside chicken. Dilute molasses with 2 tbsp boiling water and rub over surface of chicken.

3. Heat 3 tbsp oil. Fry chicken until skin is golden and meat is done. Add 3 tbsp sake and 4 tbsp boiling water. Cover and steam chicken briefly. Add 1 tbsp peanut oil.

4. Cutting through bone, divide into small serving pieces.

Peking Duck with Mandarin Pancakes

(4 servings)

INGREDIENTS

1 duckling (3 to 5 lbs)
1 tbsp salt
3 tbsp sake
¼ cup maple syrup
1 tbsp chopped parsley

½ cup hoisin sauce (see p. 199)
4 to 6 green onions cut into
    2-inch julienne strips
3 tbsp soy sauce

PREPARATION

1. Rinse and thoroughly clean duckling. If it is frozen, it must be

thoroughly thawed. Drain well. Bring about 4 cups of water to a boil and pour this over the bird to blanch the skin. Dry well inside and outside with a towel. Rub body cavity with salt, sake, and soy sauce.

2. Generously brush the duckling skin with maple syrup. Hang to dry for 4 hours.

3. Preheat oven to 175 degrees. Roast the duckling for $1\frac{1}{2}$ hours in this slow oven. Raise temperature to 325 degrees, turn the duckling breast-side down and roast for another $1\frac{1}{2}$ hours. By this time the bird should be well done and the skin crisp and golden. Remove to a serving plate. Garnish with parsley. Put the green onions on a separate serving dish, and the hoisin sauce in a serving bowl. The duckling must be carved into small thin rectangles at the table. Each guest takes a portion of the meat, some hoisin sauce, and a section of onion and wraps them in a mandarin pancake (see below).

Mandarin Pancakes

(4 servings)

INGREDIENTS

$2\frac{1}{2}$ cups all-purpose flour
1 tsp salt

1 cup boiling water
sesame oil

PREPARATION

1. Sift together flour and salt. Gradually add boiling water to make a soft dough. Cover with a towel and rest for 30 minutes.

2. Turn the dough out on a lightly floured board and knead till it is soft and smooth (about 10 minutes). Shape the dough into a long cylinder about 16 inches long and $2\frac{1}{2}$ inches in diameter. Cut the cylinder into 16 equal pieces and roll each into a ball. Flatten each ball into a circle (about 5 inches in diameter). Brush the tops of half of the pancakes with sesame oil and top each with an unoiled cake until there and 8 2-layer pancakes. Working from the center outward, roll these double cakes until they are very thin. Take care to keep the edges even.

3. Heat an unoiled heavy skillet over a medium heat. Cook each side of the pancakes about 2 or 3 minutes or until lightly browned. When all the pancakes are done separate the layers to make sixteen very thin cakes.

4. Bring about 4 cups of water to a boil in the bottom of a steamer.

Place the pancakes in the upper section and steam for about 1 minute. Remove and fold each pancake in quarters as for crepês suzette. Serve with the duck prepared as described above.

Fried Egg Rolls

(6 servings)

INGREDIENTS

1 can flaked salmon or 1 lb
    ground pork
1 tsp cornstarch
½ tsp salt
½ tsp sugar
1 tbsp soy sauce
1 tbsp cooking oil

2 sliced green onions
2 cups bean sprouts (1-lb can)
4 dried shiitake mushrooms
    soaked and shredded
1 piece minced preserved
    ginger root
½ cut chopped water chestnuts
18 Chinese pancakes (see below)

PANCAKES INGREDIENTS

1 cup flour
1 cup ice water

2 lightly beaten eggs
½ tsp salt

Combine and lightly blend the ingredients to make a thin batter. Heat a 6-inch frying pan. Brush it lightly with oil. Pour about 2 tbsp of batter into the heated pan and rotate it to cover the entire bottom evenly. Barely dry the cake over a moderate heat for about 30 seconds. Bake on one side only. Shake cake out on a damp towel and continue cooking until all the batter has been used. Cover the cakes with a towel until ready for use. You should have about 18 cakes. (It is sometimes possible to buy these cakes already prepared at oriental food stores.)

FILLING

1. In a small bowl combine flaked salmon (or pork), salt, sugar, and soy sauce.

2. Heat 1 tbsp cooking oil in a skillet and sauté the green onions lightly. Add the other filling ingredients and sauté for 2 minutes. Add the salmon mixture. Mix lightly. Chill the filling well.

3. Spread a pancake flat on a working surface. On the upper half of the cake spread 1 tbsp of the chilled filling. Fold the lower half of the

cake up to cover the filling. Fold the ends in and roll the cake into a small cylinder. Continue until you have made 18 rolls.

4. Heat about 1 inch of cooking oil in a skillet to 350 degrees. Fry the rolls for about 3 minutes, or until golden brown on all sides. Turn only once. Drain, and serve hot with the following sauce.

SWEET-AND-SOUR SAUCE
(about 1⅓ cups)
1 large dried shiitake mushroom softened in water and chopped
2 tbsp chopped green onion
2 tbsp chopped mixed sweet pickled cucumber
2 tbsp cornstarch
½ cup vinegar
½ cup water
⅓ cup sugar

Combine in a saucepan chopped mushroom, green onion, and pickle. Blend cornstarch and vinegar to form a smooth paste. Add the remaining ingredients and combine with the chopped vegetables in the saucepan. Stirring occasionally, cook over a moderate heat until thick.

Deep-fried Filled Dumplings

(4 servings)

FILLING

1 can flaked tuna
3 tsp minced dried shrimp
1 chopped green onion
1½–3 tbsp soy sauce
½ tsp salt
½ tsp monosodium glutamate

3 tsp minced water chestnuts
1 medium bamboo shoot minced
6 dried shiitake mushrooms
    soaked and minced
1 tbsp sake or dry sherry
3 tbsp oil for frying

DOUGH ———

3 cups flour (preferably sweet rice flour)
1 tsp sugar

1½ cups boiling water
oil for deep frying

PREPARATION

1. Prepare filling by combining all ingredients and stir-frying them quickly in heated oil.

2. Make pastry by combining sugar and flour, adding boiling water to make a soft dough, and covering the dough with a damp cloth. Allow it to stand for 10 minutes. Turn the dough out on a lightly floured board. Shape it into a long thin sausage shape. Cut this sausage into 1½-inch lengths and roll each slice into a thin circular cake.

3. In the center of each cake, place 1 tsp of filling. Fold the cake over the filling to form a crescent. Crimp the edges securely.

4. Fry the dumplings in about 3 cups of oil heated to 350 degrees until they are a delicate brown.

Chestnuts and Chicken

(4 servings)

INGREDIENTS

½ lb chicken breasts
10–12 chestnuts
2 tbsp oil

20 gingko nuts
1 egg white
1 tsp cornstarch

SEASONINGS A

1 tsp ginger juice
1 tsp sake
⅛ tsp salt

⅛ tsp monosodium glutamate
⅛ tsp pepper

SEASONINGS B

1½ tbsp sake
2 tbsp chicken stock or broth
1 tbsp oyster sauce (see p. 202)
⅛ tsp sesame oil

½ tsp cornstarch mixed with
  1 tbsp water
½ tsp soy sauce
1 tbsp sugar

PREPARATION

1. Slice chicken very thin. Mix with seasonings A and marinate for 10 minutes.

2. Boil chestnuts in slightly salted water for 10 minutes. Drain. Remove hulls and inner skins.

3. Heat skillet; add oil. Beat egg white until stiff, fold cornstarch into egg white. Coat marinated chicken with cornstarch and egg white. When oil is very hot (400°F), add chicken. Remove from heat and stir gently for 30 seconds. Remove chicken from skillet.

4. Add 2 tbsp more oil to skillet. Add chestnuts and gingko nuts and cook over low heat for 10 minutes. Raise heat and fry vigorously

for 1 minute. This makes nuts crispy.

5. Return chicken to skillet, add ingredients B, and simmer until sauce is thick and clear.

Steamed Transparent Dumplings

(about 24 dumplings)

INGREDIENTS

DOUGH

1 lb sifted all-purpose flour
3–4 cups boiling water

$\frac{1}{4}$ cup salad oil

FILLING

$\frac{1}{2}$ lb lean pork ground fine
$\frac{1}{2}$ lb shelled shrimps
$\frac{1}{2}$ lb Chinese cabbage or Chinese
   chard
1 small piece bamboo shoot
3 green onions minced
4 dried shiitake mushrooms
1 small section ginger root
   peeled and grated

$\frac{1}{2}$ tsp dry sherry
$1\frac{1}{2}$ tbsp soy sauce
$\frac{1}{2}$ tbsp sesame oil
1 tsp sugar
1 tsp salt
$\frac{1}{2}$ tsp white pepper
$\frac{1}{4}$ tsp monosodium glutamate

PREPARATION

DOUGH

1. In a large mixing bowl, using either your hands or a large wooden spoon, gradually combine flour and 3 cups boiling water. Blend mixture to form a firm, nonadhering paste. (Add more boiling water if necessary.) Cover bowl with a damp cloth and let the dough rest for 30 minutes.

2. Place dough on a lightly floured pastry board and knead it for 5 minutes. Divide the dough into two parts. Return half of dough to the bowl and cover it with damp cloth. Shape the other half into a cylinder about 1 inch in diameter.

3. Oil a sharp knife or cleaver and cut the sausage-shaped dough into pieces $\frac{3}{4}$ inch long. Cover pieces of dough with damp cloth. Roll each piece into a ball. Then flatten each ball with palm of hand. Next roll each flat piece with a rolling pin into a sheet $3\frac{1}{2}$ inches in diameter and $\frac{1}{8}$ inch thick. Cover with kitchen wrap or dry cloth.

1. Wash and parboil the Chinese cabbage. Then mince it and pat dry with paper towels. Sprinkle the mushrooms with 1 tsp sugar and soak in water to cover for 30 minutes. Drain mushrooms; cut off and discard stems. After cutting them into long, thin strips, mince the mushrooms. Mince bamboo shoot.

2. Rinse, shell, and devein shrimp. Wash under cold running water. Drain well and pat dry with paper; mince them. Add pork and continue mincing until the meat is reduced almost to a paste and is thoroughly combined with shrimp. In a mixing bowl combine meat and shrimp mixture with Chinese cabbage, bamboo shoot, green onion, mushrooms, and grated ginger. Add sherry, soy sauce, sesame oil, sugar, salt, pepper, and monosodium glutamate. Blend thoroughly.

North-China dumplings may be made in either of the following two ways.

1. Half-moon shape. Place 2 tsp of filling in the center of round sheet of dough and fold the round in half to make a half-moon shape. Pinch edges to seal. This is a plain half-moon dumpling.

2. Bonnet-shape. Crook index finger of right hand against the center of a flat circle of dough; this place will eventually form the pouch containing the filling. Pleat $\frac{2}{3}$ of the edge by making 6 or 7 small, even folds along the edge. Fill the pouch with 2 tsp of filling. Pleat the remaining $\frac{1}{3}$ of the edge to enclose the filling completely.

3. These dumplings are usually steamed and are often the main dish of a meal in northern China. The finished pastry is shiny, slightly translucent, and chewy. Before steaming, coat each dumpling lightly with oil. Place on a heatproof dish in the top section of a steamer and steam for 15 minutes. Arrange the steamed dumplings on a heated platter and serve with a dip made of soy sauce and vinegar.

Fried Transparent Dumplings

INGREDIENTS
Dough and Filling
See dough and filling for Steamed Transparent Dumplings, p. 52.

PREPARATION
1. Prepare bonnet-shaped dumplings, p. 52.

2. Heat about 1 tbsp of oil in skillet, place dumplings gently in the pan. Cook over low heat for 2 minutes or until the bottoms brown lightly.

3. Add $\frac{1}{2}$ cup of cold water, cover the skillet, and cook over moderate heat for about 12–13 minutes or until all the liquid has evaporated. Serve dumplings on a heated platter browned side up. Accompany them with soy sauce and vinegar dip.

Steamed Buns with Roast-pork Filling

(30 buns)

INGREDIENTS

STEAMED-BREAD DOUGH

2 cakes compressed or 2 pkg dry yeast

$\frac{1}{2}$ cup lukewarm water

$1\frac{1}{2}$ cups scalded milk

$\frac{1}{2}$ cup sugar

$2\frac{1}{2}$ tsp salt

$\frac{3}{4}$ cup shortening or butter

$4\frac{1}{2}$–5 cups sifted all-purpose flour

1 egg beaten

$\frac{1}{4}$ cup melted shortening

FILLING

1 pound Chinese roast pork

2 tbsp soy sauce

$\frac{1}{2}$ tsp sugar

$\frac{1}{2}$ tsp salt

pepper

1 tbsp cornstarch

2 tbsp sesame seeds

$\frac{1}{2}$ tbsp salad oil

30 2-inch squares of wax paper

PREPARATION

1. Soften yeast in likewarm water. (Dry yeast requires warmer water.)

2. Combine milk, sugar, salt, and shortening or butter. Mix well.

3. When milk mixture is lukewarm, add yeast and 3 cups flour. Beat thoroughly (2 minutes with electric beater). Cover and let rise until light.

4. Punch the dough down and add well beaten egg and enough flour (about 2 cups) to make a dough stiff enough to knead. Turn out on a lightly floured board, knead until smooth (about 10 minutes), brush lightly with melted shortening. Place dough in a large bowl, cover, and let rise in a warm, draftless place until double in size (about 1 hour).

5. Punch dough down. Cover and let rest 20 minutes. Divide dough

in half. On a lightly floured surface form each half into a long sausage-like shape about 2 inches in diameter. Oil the blade of cleaver and cut off pieces of dough about 1 inch long. Roll each piece into a ball. Cover pieces with a damp cloth.

FILLING

1. Dice Chinese roast pork. Combine the pork with soy sauce, sugar, salt, and pepper and marinate for a few minutes.

2. Parch sesame seeds to a golden brown over extremely low fire. Add them to meat mixture. Dissolve cornstarch in 2 tbsp water. Add to meat mixture. Heat oil in a skillet and add pork mixture. Cook until the mixture thickens and the pork is covered with a clear glaze. Remove from heat and set aside.

3. Flatten each piece of dough with the palm of the hand. Then with blade of a cleaver shape it into a circle 4 inches in diameter. Put 2 tbsp of filling in the center of each round and fold dough over, turning the rim upward until it completely encloses the fillings. Leave a small opening at top center. Finally close this opening by pinching the edges together.

4. Place the buns on wax-paper squares, cover with cloth, let rise for about 30 minutes, then steam in the top section of a steamer for 10 minutes. Serve hot.

Fried Noodles with Assorted Meats

(8 servings)

INGREDIENTS

¾ lb Chinese noodles
½ cup oil
¼ tsp fresh ginger finely sliced
¼ lb pork
¼ lb chicken breasts skinned, boned, and cut into julienne strips
2 abalone sliced

1 green onion
1 onion sliced
4 dried shiitake mushrooms soaked and sliced
1 medium bamboo shoot
1 lb bean sprouts
¼ pkg kikurage (see p. 200) soaked and sliced
½ stalk celery

4 oz fresh snow peas parboiled and sliced in strips
$\frac{1}{4}$ lb ham sliced in strips
Chinese roast pork sliced in strips
egg strips (see p. 106)
1 loaf kamaboko (see p. 200) sliced

SEASONINGS A

$\frac{1}{2}$ tsp soy sauce

$\frac{1}{8}$ tsp salt

$\frac{1}{2}$ tsp sake or dry sherry

$\frac{1}{8}$ tsp monosodium glutamate

SEASONINGS B

1 cup chicken stock

$1\frac{1}{2}$ tsp cornstarch mixed
with 1 tbsp water

$\frac{1}{3}$ cup sake or dry sherry

$\frac{1}{4}$ cup soy sauce

$\frac{1}{4}$ tsp monosodium glutamate

$\frac{1}{2}$ tsp salt

PREPARATION

1. Fry noodles in $\frac{1}{4}$ cup hot oil until light brown. Drain and set aside.

2. Heat remaining oil in large skillet. Add ginger and fry until light brown; remove from oil and discard.

3. Add seasoning A, sauté pork, onion, and green onion in ginger flavored oil.

4. Heat 1 tbsp oil over high heat until very hot, add mushrooms, bamboo shoot, kikurage, and celery. Sauté. Rinse bean sprouts under running cold water; drain and sauté.

5. Add remaining ingredients and seasonings B. Simmer 5 minutes. Blend with noodles. Sprinkle ham and finely shredded roast pork on top of noodle mixture. Remove to large platter. Garnish with snow peas, egg strips, and kamaboko.

Chinese Noodles in Broth 1

(1 serving)

INGREDIENTS

1 pkg Chinese noodles

2 slices Chinese roast pork

1 medium bamboo shoot

1 green onion chopped

2 tbsp soy sauce
$\frac{1}{2}$ tbsp vinegar
$\frac{1}{2}$ tbsp sugar

dash salt
dash monosodium glutamate

SOUP

1 lb chicken bones
1 lb pork bones
1 green onion

4 slices ginger
10 cups water

PREPARATION

1. Heat skillet; add 1 tbsp oil and bamboo shoots. Add 1 tbsp soy sauce, $\frac{1}{2}$ tbsp vinegar, and $\frac{1}{2}$ tbsp sugar. Simmer until all the liquid is absorbed by the bamboo shoots.

2. To make soup stock, combine in a large kettle chicken bones, pork bones, sliced green onion, ginger, and 10 cups of cold water. Bring to a boil; remove scum that forms on top. Simmer covered for from 40 minutes to 1 hour. Strain.

3. Meanwhile, in soup bowl, combine 1 tbsp soy sauce and a dash of monosodium glutamate and salt.

4. In medium kettle, cook noodles as package label directs. Rinse under running cold water.

5. Put into soup bowl (step 3) chopped green onion, soup stock, and noodles.

6. Arrange bamboo shoot and of pork on top and sprinkle with pepper.

Chinese Noodles in Broth 2

(4 servings)

INGREDIENTS

4 pkg Chinese noodles
$\frac{1}{2}$ lb pork finely shredded
2 dried shiitake mushrooms
2 green onions
2 tsp salt
2 leaves Chinese cabbage shredded
2 tbsp soy sauce

1 additional tsp soy sauce
1 tsp sake
1 additional tbsp sake
pepper
dash of monosodium glutamate
2 tbsp salad oil
6 cups boiling water

PREPARATION

1. In small bowl combine shredded pork, 1 tsp soy sauce, and 1 tsp sake.

2. Soak mushrooms till soft, drain, and cut into quarters. Cut green onion into ¼-inch slices.

3. Heat skillet. Add 2 tbsp salad oil and heat till very hot. Sauté mushrooms, pork, green onion, and Chinese cabbage. Combine 2 tbsp soy sauce, and 6 cups boiling water. To this add 2 tsp salt, monosodium glutamate, pepper, and 1 tbsp sake.

4. Boil Chinese noodles as package label directs; rinse under running cold water. Combine noodles with soup and all other ingredients.

Egg-flower Soup

(4–5 servings)

INGREDIENTS

1 egg well beaten
1 green onion
1 sheet dried laver cut into
   1½-inch squares
½ fresh ginger root grated

1 tbsp cornstarch mixed with
   3 tbsp water
4 cups soup stock No. 1 (p. 69)
1 tsp salt
1 tsp soy sauce
dash monosodium glutamate

PREPARATION

1. Dilute well beaten egg with an equal volume of water. Mix well.

2. Add soy sauce, monosodium glutamate and salt to soup stock and bring to a boil.

3. Add cornstarch and water to soup and mix. Bring to a boil.

4. Pour egg mixture slowly on the surface of the boiling soup; the egg will float and form threads.

5. Pour soup into individual bowls. Garnish with laver, grated ginger, and green onions.

Abalone Soup

(4 servings)

INGREDIENTS

½ can abalone
4 dried shiitake mushrooms
2 slices smoked ham

1 tbsp vegetable oil
1 tsp cornstarch
1 tbsp soy sauce

2 oz lean pork	1 tsp sherry
8 snow peas	$\frac{1}{2}$ tsp sugar
2 thin slices fresh ginger	2 tsp salt
6 cups chicken stock	$\frac{1}{2}$ tsp monosodium glutamate

PREPARATION

1. Soak mushrooms in water for 30 minutes. Discard stems and mince caps. Slice abalone and ham into julienne strips. Slice the pork and combine it with cornstarch, soy sauce, sugar, and sherry.

2. Cut off ends of snow peas and blanch for 1 minute.

3. Heat oil in a deep pot. Fry ginger slices and salt for $\frac{1}{2}$ minute then pour in stock. Bring the stock to a boil, add mushrooms, and pork mixture. Cover pot and simmer for 5 minutes.

4. Add abalone, ham, and snow peas; simmer for 1 minute. Add monosodium glutamate. Before serving, remove and discard ginger slices.

Sour-and-hot Soup

(4 servings)

INGREDIENTS

4 large dried shiitake mushrooms	$1\frac{1}{2}$ tbsp white vinegar
$\frac{1}{2}$ cup canned bamboo shoots	1 tbsp cornstarch mixed
$\frac{1}{4}$ pound lean pork	with 3 tbsp water
3 cups chicken stock	1 egg lightly beaten
$\frac{1}{2}$ tsp white pepper	1 green onion, including the
$\frac{1}{2}$ tsp monosodium glutamate	green part, minced
1 tsp sesame oil	1 tsp sugar
$1\frac{1}{2}$ tbsp soy sauce	dash salt

PREPARATION

1. Sprinkle 1 tsp sugar on the dried mushrooms and soak in $\frac{1}{2}$ cup water for at least 30 minutes. Squeeze them; remove and discard stems. Cut caps into paper-thin slices and then into thin strips.

2. Drain the bamboo shoot and cut into julienne strips.

3. Slice pork very thin and cut slices into narrow strips about 2 inches long.

4. Bring chicken stock to a boil. Add mushrooms, bamboo shoots, and pork. Cook for 3 minutes.

5. Add soy sauce, vinegar, pepper, and cornstarch mixture. Stir for a few seconds until the soup thickens. Then slowly pour in beaten egg, stir, and add monosodium glutamate. Remove soup from heat.

6. Add salt to taste and stir in the sesame oil. Sprinkle the top with green onion. Serve immediately.

Winter-melon Soup

(4 to 6 servings)

INGREDIENTS

1 winter melon (about 4 lbs)
½ cup lotus seeds (see p. 201)
4 dried shiitake mushrooms
½ cup bamboo shoots sliced thin
½ cup abalone shredded
4 chicken breasts shredded
2 thin slices fresh ginger root
   minced

2 tbsp sake or dry sherry
1 tsp sugar
1½ tsp salt
¼ tsp white pepper
2 slices smoked ham
¼ tsp monosodium glutamate
8 cups chicken stock
1½ tbsp oil

PREPARATION

1. Soak mushrooms until soft, remove and discard stems, and then slice caps thin. Dice bamboo shoots.

2. Cut off top of melon (about ¼ of the way from the top) and scrape out pulp and seeds. Reserve top.

3. Boil lotus seeds for 10 minutes and remove brown husks. Add lotus seeds and sliced mushrooms to winter melon.

4. Put the winter melon in top of a large steamer. Pour chicken stock into winter melon until it is ⅔ full, add 1 tsp salt, and cover with melon top. Steam 3 to 5 hours or until winter melon meat is translucent and tender.

5. Combine sherry, sugar, ½ tsp salt, and pepper, and shredded raw chicken. Heat 1½ tbsp oil in a skillet and sauté minced ginger and chicken until lightly browned. In the top of a double boiler combine 2 cups chicken stock and sautéed chicken. Simmer covered for 3 hours. Add this concentrated soup to contents of winter melon.

6. Five minutes before serving, add slices of bamboo shoot, shredded ham, and sliced abalone. Season with monosodium glutamate.

7. Remove melon carefully to a serving bowl. Scoop out soup and some of the melon for each portion. When 2 or 3 inches of melon have been scooped out, cut away peel to make serving easier.

Bird's Nest Soup

(4 to 6 servings)

INGREDIENTS

1½ oz dried bird's nest (see p. 196)
8 cups chicken broth
2 chicken breasts
3 egg whites beaten

2 tbsp cornstarch
2 tsp salt
¼ lb smoked ham in julienne strips
½ tsp monosodium glutamate

PREPARATION

1. Put dried bird's nest in 1 pint boiling water. Soak them overnight. Drain off water and place the softened nests in a large pan. Add 3 cups hot water and simmer 30 minutes. Then place in a bowl and set aside to cool.

2. Chill 1 cup of chicken broth.

3. Mince chicken breast to a pulp. Slowly stir in chilled chicken broth and continue stirring with chopsticks. Strands of muscle will cling to the tips of the chopsticks; these must be discarded.

4. Add the beaten egg whites into the chicken pulp mixture.

5. 15 minutes before serving, combine bird's nest and chicken broth in a 3-quart saucepan. Dissolve cornstarch in 2 tbsp water and add to chicken broth to thicken the soup. Bring to a boil over high heat then immediately reduce the heat to low and simmer. Add the ham, salt and monosodium glutamate. Just before serving, remove soup from the fire and slowly stir in chicken pulp and egg white.

Chicken Soup with Green Beans

(4 servings)

INGREDIENTS

4 chicken breasts boned and
  minced

1 head Chinese cabbage cut into
  bite-size pieces

½ cup green beans washed and
cut into 1-inch lengths
4 cups stock

½ cup thinly sliced mushrooms
cornstarch for dredging

SEASONINGS A
4 tbsp water
1 tsp salt
dash pepper
dash monosodium glutamate

2 tbsp sake
2 tbsp cornstarch
2 egg whites lightly beaten

SEASONINGS B
dash salt

dash monosodium glutamate
½ tsp sake

PREPARATION

1. Combine minced chicken meat with 4 tbsp water. Add seasonings A and mix well.

2. Dredge the green beans in cornstarch.

3. Parboil the beans for about 2 minutes and plunge immediately into cold water to arrest cooking.

4. Heat 4 cups of stock in a saucepan. Add the chicken mixture, Chinese cabbage, beans, and mushrooms. Bring to a boil, reduce heat, and simmer till the chicken is done and the vegetables tender. Add seasonings B. Serve hot.

Vegetable Variety Soup

(6 servings)

INGREDIENTS
1 carrot
1 bamboo shoot
1 cucumber
1 potato
2 turnips
15 gingko nuts
3 dried shiitake mushrooms
or ½ cup sliced mushrooms

5 or 6 boiled and shelled quail
eggs
½ head Chinese cabbage
½ cup snow peas
2 spears fresh asparagus
stock to cover vegetables

62

dash salt   1 tsp chicken fat or clarified butter
1 tsp cornstarch dissolved in
  1 tsp water

PREPARATION

1. After cleaning all the vegetables, cut them into attractive, uniform pieces.

2. Bring the stock to a boil, reduce heat, and simmer. Add vegetables, beginning with the toughest and adding the tender cabbage and snow peas last.

3. Season to taste. Pour into a serving tureen and add 1 tsp chicken fat or clarified butter. Serve hot.

Steamed Rice with Chinese Sausage

(4 servings)

INGREDIENTS

2 cups long-grain rice   4 Chinese sausages
4 cups water   ½ tsp butter

PREPARATION

1. Wash rice 3 or 4 times, rubbing gently between hands till the rinsing water runs clear. Drain very well.

2. Combine rice and water in a heavy, 2-quart saucepan, bring water to a boil, drop in ½ tsp butter to prevent the rice from boiling over. Reduce heat to low and add Chinese sausage, which is available in most oriental markets. Cover the pan tightly. Without stirring allow rice to cook slowly undisturbed for 20 minutes.

3. Turn off heat, but do not remove the lid. Let the rice steam for 15 minutes. If the rice on top is flaky and cooked through and if natural steam holes are formed in the surface, the rice is ready. Serve hot topped with sausage. This dish is usually served with a soup.

Fried Rice

(4 to 8 servings)

INGREDIENTS

¼ pound chicken meat   2 tbsp soy sauce
  (1 breast) cooked and diced   1 tsp salt

¼ pound roast pork diced
¼ pound shrimp shelled and
  cleaned
4 dried shiitake mushrooms
  soaked and sliced
3 eggs
4 green onions

¼ tsp pepper
¼ cup salad oil
2 tbsp butter or margarine
2 tbsp sake or dry sherry
4 cups boiled rice at least
  one day old

PREPARATION

1. Heat 2 tbsp butter or margarine in a skillet. Add shrimp and fry quickly. Add remaining meats and mushrooms. Sauté 2 minutes, remove from skillet, and set aside.

2. Heat salad oil in skillet, toss in rice. Fry rice until hot, stirring and pressing to break up limps. Add salt, sake, pepper, shrimps, meats and mushrooms.

3. When thoroughly mixed, make a hollow in the center of the rice, break in eggs and scramble. Stir into rice mixture and sauté 2 or 3 minutes.

4. Stir in green onion, sprinkle with soy sauce, season to taste, and serve.

Pork Congee

(4 servings)

INGREDIENTS

1½ cups raw rice
1 gallon water
½ lb pork loin minced
2 tbsp oil
1 small piece of ginger root
  sliced thin
1 piece dried tangerine skin

1 bunch parsley leaves minced
2 green onions minced
1 small piece pickled cabbage
  finely chopped
1 tsp sugar
2 tsp salt
½ tsp white pepper

PREPARATION

1. Wash rice thoroughly and drain. Heat water in a heavy pan. Bring to a boil, add rice, 1 tbsp oil, and 2 tsp salt. Cook uncovered for 30 minutes.

2. After 30 minutes, add dried tangerine skin and ginger, cover pot and simmer for 1½ hours.

3. Add minced pork, 1 tbsp oil, sugar, pepper, and minced pickled cabbage. Simmer 20 minutes. Five minutes before serving, sprinkle with chopped green onion and parsley leaves.

Roast Duck Congee

(4 servings)

INGREDIENTS

1½ cups raw rice
1 roast duck (including bones, legs, wings, neck)
3 dried scallops
1 small piece dried tangerine skin
1 gallon water

2 tbsp salad oil
1 tbsp salt
1 small piece ginger root sliced thin
2 green onions minced
1 bunch parsley leaves minced

PREPARATION

1. Wash rice thoroughly and drain. Combine 1 gallon of water with dried scallops. Bring to a boil, add rice, oil, tangerine skin and salt. Cook uncovered for 30 minutes.

2. Add duck and ginger. Cover pot and simmer for 1½ to 2 hours.

3. Five minutes before serving, sprinkle with chopped green onion and parsley.

Chinese Rice Pudding

(6 servings)

INGREDIENTS

1½ cups steamed glutinous or other rice
1 cup sugar
3 tbsp lard or other unseasoned shortening
½ cup sweetened bean paste or puréed fruit
1 or 2 pieces crystallized orange rind cut into fancy shapes

3 plums pitted and quartered
1 slice firm melon cut into fancy shapes
5 or 6 dates
2 or 3 slices canned pineapple
4 or 5 canned pitted cherries
¼ cup raisins
1 cup heavy sugar syrup

The shapes you choose for the fruits depend on the ornamental pattern you intend to use on the top of the pudding. You may vary the designs and the ingredients to suit your own tastes.

1. Grease the inside of a deep bowl and make a pattern in it with the prepared fruits.

2. The rice must be warm. Combine it with 1 cup of sugar and mix well.

3. Gently pack about half of the sweetened rice on top of the fruits, taking care not to disturb the pattern.

4. Make a well in the center of the rice and fill it with sweetened bean paste or stiff puréed fruit. Cover this with the remaining rice.

5. Bring water to a boil in the bottom of a steamer. Place the pudding in the top of the steamer, cover, and steam for about 1 hour. Or set the bowl in a pan of hot water, and bake it in a 300-degree oven for 30 minutes.

6. Invert the pudding on a serving dish and remove the bowl.

7. Cover the pudding with sugar syrup just before serving.

Fruit Cocktail in Syrup

(6 servings)

INGREDIENTS

2 tbsp almond paste or 1
   tsp almond extract
1 heaping tsp flour
6 tbsp milk

3 cups water
1½ cups water
1½ cups sugar
2 cups canned fruit cocktail

PREPARATION

1. In a saucepan combine 3 cups water with 1½ cups sugar. Bring to a boil. Remove from heat and stir until sugar is completely dissolved.

2. Combine flour with almond paste and water to make a smooth mixture. Add milk.

3. Combining this mixture with the syrup must be done carefully to avoid lumping. Submerge a ladle only to its upper edge in the sugar syrup. Pour the almond-paste mixture into the ladle and swirl it gently to distribute it evenly throughout the syrup.

4. Spoon canned fruit cocktail into individual serving dishes and top it with the almond flavored syrup.

Japan

During the past century, Japanese eating habits have changed vastly. Meats and dairy products are now consumed in large quantities, whereas in ancient Japan rice, seafoods, and vegetables—especially beans— were the staples of the diets of everyone from the loftiest nobles to the humblest peasants. Old ways cannot be completely uprooted, however, and fresh fish, shellfish, lightly cooked vegetables, and, of course, rice in a wide variety of dishes remain great favorites. In this book I have tried to give a sampling of many Japanese dishes because too often peoples of the West consider sukiyaki and tempura all there is to the national diet. I have included several recipes for one-dish casserole meals because they are generally easy to prepare, nutritious, and conducive to good fellowship since traditionally the whole family eats from the deep dish in which the ingredients are cooked. I have limited the number of noodle dishes, although the Japanese are very fond of them, for two reasons. First, many of the noodle recipes widely used in Japan are basically Chinese; consequently, I have put them in the Chinese section of the book. Second, it is an easy matter to use the Japanese noodle recipe given here in a number of different ways simply by varying the garnishes.

Sushi, which occurs in various guises but always calls for the vinegared rice that gives the genre its name, ought to better known in the West. In Japan it is a luxury food most often eaten in restaurants, but by following the detailed instructions in this book, anyone can add it to their domestic cuisine. Two very important things to remember about all Japanese foods are that they demand the best quality ingredients— especially dishes calling for seafoods—and that they are always served attractively, for the Japanese consider the appearance of the dish integral to its taste appeal.

Soups

Soup Stocks

SOUP STOCK NO. 1
This is a basic, clear soup stock.

4 cups water
4 square inches dried kelp
  (see seaweeds, p. 204)

2 cups katsuobushi (shavings
  of dried bonito; see p. 200)
½ tsp salt

PREPARATION

1. Wash kelp with cool water and place in large pot. Cover with 4 cups water and bring to boil over low heat. Remove kelp and reserve for use in Soup Stock No. 2.

2. Add shaved dried bonito and bring to boil; turn heat off at once.

3. After a few of minutes of steeping, the bonito shavings will settle to the bottom. Strain the stock through a fine sieve or piece of cheesecloth into another pot. Reserve bonito for use in Soup Stock No. 2.

SOUP STOCK NO. 2
This is used as stock for vegetable or meat dishes.

1. Cover kelp and bonito shavings from soup No. 1 with 4 cups of fresh water. Bring to boil and simmer for 5 minutes.

2. Remove from heat and strain after everything has settled to the bottom.

Bean-paste Soup with Bean Curd

(5 servings)

INGREDIENTS

½ cup bean paste
1 cake bean curd
7 cups stock (see p 69)
3 green onions chopped

1 cake fried bean curd
  (aburaage; see p. 195, bean
  curd)
1 tsp monosodium glutamate

1. Dissolve bean paste in stock, add monosodium glutamate, and bring to a boil.

2. Cut bean curd and fried bean curd into bite-size pieces. Add to boiling bean-paste soup.

3. Pour into soup bowls and garnish with chopped green onions.

Bean-paste Soup with Vegetables

(4 servings)

INGREDIENTS

1 stalk burdock	1 tbsp oil
1 carrot	8 cups stock No. 2 (p. 69)
4 dried shiitake mushrooms	4 tbsp any bean paste
1 green onion	2 tsp grated ginger
1 cake fried bean curd (aburaage; see p. 195)	dash Japanese pepper
	$\frac{1}{2}$ tsp monosodium glutamate
1 lb chicken meat	

PREPARATION

1. Cut burdock and carrot into bite-size pieces. Soak mushrooms in water. When soft, remove and discard stems, and slice caps. Cut green onion and aburaage into short lengths. Dice chicken meat. Heat oil in a frying pan. Sauté chicken briefly. Add burdock, carrot, mushrooms, green onion, and stock.

2. Simmer chicken and vegetables over low heat. Degrease if necessary. Continue cooking until vegetables are tender. Add bean paste, monosodium glutamate, and green onion.

3. Add ginger and Japanese pepper, if available. Serve in individual bowls with plenty of soup poured over vegetables.

Clear Chicken Soup

(4 servings)

INGREDIENTS

$\frac{1}{3}$ lb chicken or half a large breast

2 dried shiitake mushrooms
8 pieces fish loaf (kamaboko;
  see p. 200)
2 green onions
1 ginger root
cornstarch for dredging

4 cups soup stock No. 1 (p. 69)
1 tsp salt
1 tsp soy sauce
2 tbsp sake or dry sherry
$\frac{1}{4}$ tsp monosodium glutamate
salt and sake for step 1

PREPARATION

1. Cut chicken in thin, 1-inch-long pieces and sprinkle it lightly with salt and sake. Rub cornstarch into chicken then place it in bamboo basket or large strainer and lower twice into very hot water. Take out and cool. Cut fish loaf (kamaboko) into flower-shapes. Using only the white part of the green onion, cut it and the ginger in 1-inch julienne strips. Soak in cold water. Soak mushrooms in water till soft. Drain, remove and discard stems, and cut caps in strips.

2. Place soup stock No. 1 in pot and bring to a boil. Add 1 tsp salt, soy sauce, 2 tbsp sake, and monosodium glutamate. Add chicken and mushrooms. Simmer for 10 minutes. Skim off scum that forms on top.

3. Drain green onion and ginger strips; squeeze out water. Place chicken, shiitake mushrooms, fish loaf, and green onion in individual bowls. Add soup stock and garnish with ginger strips.

Japanese Sauces

The following sauces have an infinite range of uses on vegetable, meat, or fish dishes. Most of them are extremely easy to prepare: all you do is combine the ingredients.

Sweet-and-sour Sauce

INGREDIENTS

$\frac{1}{2}$ cup rice vinegar
2 tbsp sugar
$\frac{1}{2}$ tsp mirin (see p. 201)

$\frac{1}{2}$ tsp salt
$\frac{1}{4}$ tsp monosodium glutamate

PREPARATION

Simply mix the ingredients and pour them like a salad dressing over raw vegetables.

Vinegar and Soy-sauce Dressing (dark)

INGREDIENTS

½ cup rice vinegar

1 tbsp soy sauce

salt to taste

dash monosodium glutamate

PREPARATION

Simply mix the ingredients thoroughly and use as a dressing for vegetables

Vinegar and Soy-sauce Dressing (light)

INGREDIENTS

½ cup rice vinegar

1½ tbsp sugar

½ tbsp soy sauce

½ tsp salt

¼ tsp monosodium glutamate

PREPARATION

Combine the ingredients thoroughly and use as a dressing for vegetables or fish salads.

Sesame and Vinegar Dressing

INGREDIENTS

3 tbsp white sesame seeds

3 tbsp rice vinegar

1 tbsp sugar

¼ tsp salt

¼ tsp monosodium glutamate

PREPARATION

1. Parch the seeds in a skillet. Shake constantly to prevent sticking and scorching. When they are fragrant and begin to pop like popcorn they are ready.

2. Grind the parched seeds to a paste in a mortar or an electric blender. Continuing to grind, add the other ingredients.

3. When all ingredients are thoroughly mixed, use the dressing on fish or shellfish.

Sesame and Soy-sauce Dressing

INGREDIENTS

3 tbsp white sesame seeds

3 tbsp soy sauce

1½ tbsp sugar

¼ tsp monosodium glutamate

PREPARATION

1. Parch the seeds as in the preceding recipe.

2. Grind the seeds in a mortar or electric blender, gradually adding the other ingredients to form a smooth dressing.

3. Use at once on vegetables.

Bean-paste and Vinegar Dressing

INGREDIENTS

4 tbsp white bean paste

2 tbsp sugar

2 tsp mirin (see p. 201)

⅓ cup rice vinegar

PREPARATION

Combine all ingredients thoroughly and use to coat fish or shellfish.

Bean-curd Sauce

INGREDIENTS

2 tbsp white sesame seeds

⅔ block bean curd

1 tbsp sugar

1½ tsp mirin (see p. 201)

1 tsp soy sauce

⅓ tsp salt

½ tsp monosodium glutamate

PREPARATION

1. Parch sesame seeds then grind them in a mortar or electric blender.

2. Drain water from bean curd and add to seeds; continue to grind or blend to a smooth paste.

3. Add other ingredients and blend well.

4. Use on parboiled snow peas, carrots, or other vegetables.

Mustard and Bean-paste Dressing

INGREDIENTS

4 tbsp white bean paste

4–5 tbsp rice vinegar

1½ to 2 tbsp sugar

2 tsp dry mustard

PREPARATION

Mix ingredients well and use on fish.

Thickened Vinegar Sauce

INGREDIENTS

3 tbsp rice vinegar

1–1½ tbsp sugar

½ tsp salt

1 tsp cornstarch

½ cup stock

½ tsp monosodium glutamate

PREPARATION

Mix all ingredients in a saucepan, stirring to form a smooth paste. Heat till thickened and clear. Cool and serve with boiled or broiled fish, shrimp, chicken, crab, or other seafood.

Egg and Vinegar Sauce

INGREDIENTS

1–2 egg yolks lightly beaten
2 tbsp rice vinegar
1 tbsp sake
2 tsp sugar

$\frac{1}{4}$ tsp soy sauce
$\frac{1}{2}$ tsp salt
$\frac{1}{2}$ tsp monosodium glutamate

PREPARATION

1. To lightly beaten egg yolks add vinegar, sake, sugar, and salt. Over a *very* low heat, cook these ingredients, stirring constantly, until the mixture thickens. Add soy sauce and monosodium glutamate. This sauce is good on crab, chicken, shrimp, or vegetables.

Green Cucumber Sauce

INGREDIENTS

1 cucumber grated
1 tbsp rice vinegar
1 tbsp soy sauce

1 tsp sugar
$\frac{1}{2}$ tbsp sake.

PREPARATION

Simply combine the ingredients and use as a salad dressing or as a garnish for broiled meats or fish.

Vinegared Vegetables

Chicken and Cucumber Salad

(4 servings)

INGREDIENTS

$\frac{1}{2}$ chicken or 1 large chicken
   breast
3 cucumbers
1 slice boiled ham
$\frac{1}{2}$ cup rice vinegar

2 tsp salt
1 tbsp sugar
sake
ginger juice
2 tbsp sugar

$\frac{1}{2}$ tsp salt
$\frac{1}{2}$ tsp monosodium glutamate
$\frac{1}{2}$ tsp mirin (see p. 201)

GARNISHES
2 slices pineapple
4–6 cherries

PREPARATION

1. Wash chicken thoroughly. Bring water in bottom of a steamer to a boil. Sprinkle sake and ginger juice over chicken. Steam chicken in steamer for from 10 to 20 minutes. The chicken may be roasted for 1 hour at 350°. Refrigerate till thoroughly chilled. Cut into strips.

2. Cut cucumber into julienne strips and sprinkle with 2 tsp salt. Let stand for 30 minutes.

3. Rinse cucumber well. Sprinkle it with 1 tbsp sugar and allow it to stand. Cut ham into julienne strips.

4. Combine vinegar, 2 tbsp sugar, and seasonings A to make sauce.

5. Marinate cucumber, chicken, and ham in sauce.

6. Serve garnished with pineapple and cherries.

Mixed Vinegared Vegetables

(4 servings)

INGREDIENTS
1 cucumber
1 carrot
1 daikon radish
2 oz boiled ham

2 tbsp white sesame seeds
2 tsp salt
1 tbsp sugar

SAUCE
1 tbsp soy sauce
$\frac{1}{2}$ cup rice vinegar
$\frac{1}{2}$ tsp mirin (see p. 201)

dash salt
dash monosodium glutamate

PREPARATION

1. Cut cucumber, carrot, daikon radish, and ham in julienne strips 1 inch long. Sprinkle salt over vegetables and set aside for 30 minutes. Rinse vegetables. Sprinkle them with 1 tbsp sugar and set aside for 30 minutes.

2. Combine 1 tbsp soy sauce, $\frac{1}{2}$ cup vinegar, $\frac{1}{2}$ tsp mirin, and dash each of salt and monosodium glutamate.

3. Parch sesame seeds over low heat.

4. Wipe vegetables thoroughly with cloth and arrange in a bowl with the ham. Pour sauce (step 2) over them and sprinkle them with parched sesame seeds. Serve at once.

Crab with Egg-yolk Dressing

(4 servings)

INGREDIENTS

½ lb carefully cleaned, cooked crab meat
1 bunch watercress
1 beaten egg yolk
2 tbsp rice vinegar

1 tbsp sake
2 tbsp sugar
½ tsp salt
¼ tsp soy sauce
½ tsp monosodium glutamate

PREPARATION

1. Sauce. Combine egg yolk, vinegar, sake, sugar, and salt. Stir until sugar is dissolved. Then add soy sauce and monosodium glutamate.

2. Parboil watercress in water for 30 seconds. Plunge into cold water. Drain and squeeze out excess water. Slice into 1-inch lengths. Make a mound of watercress on each of 4 serving plates. Arrange crab meat around it. Pour sauce over crab and watercress.

Vinegared Chicken and Spinach

(4 servings)

INGREDIENTS

1 large chicken breast
1 bunch spinach
3 green onions
5 tbsp vinegar
6 tbsp soy sauce

½ tsp monosodium glutamate
3–4 tbsp grated daikon radish flavored with chopped chili pepper to taste

PREPARATION

1. Wash chicken thoroughly. Sprinkle it with salt and steam in a steamer for 5 minutes. Cool, skin, and bone it. Cut it into strips.

2. Place spinach in boiling water, roots downward, and parboil for 1 minute. Remove and plunge into cold water. Squeeze gently to remove moisture. Shape the spinach into a cylinder. Slice it in 1-inch lengths.

3. Wash the onions and cut them so as to divide the green part from the white. Bring ½ cup of water to a boil in a saucepan. Put the white parts of the onions into the water, cover, and boil for about 20 seconds. Add the green parts, stir to mix well, cover, and boil for an additional 30 seconds. Remove the onions, cool, and cut them into 1-inch lengths.

4. Combine vinegar, soy sauce, and monosodium glutamate. Pour this mixture over chicken and vegetables.

5. Arrange in individual dishes and garnish with grated daikon radish flavored with chopped chili pepper.

Chrysanthemum Turnips

(4 servings)

INGREDIENTS

8 to 12 small turnips
2 tbsp salmon roe broken into
   small sections
1 tsp lemon juice
1 red pepper minced

4 tbsp vinegar
1½ tbsp sugar
½ tsp salt
dash monosodium glutamate

PREPARATION

1. Peel turnips and make a checkerboard pattern of incisions over the entire upper surface. These cuts must extend only about ⅔ of the way through the turnip. Salt turnips and allow them to wilt slightly.

2. Combine vinegar, sugar, salt, monosodium glutamate, and minced red pepper.

3. Wash turnips, squeeze them, and marinate in the vinegar and sugar mixture overnight or for at least 12 hours. Remove from the marinade and squeeze out moisture. The cut turnips should open like flowers. Sprinkle the broken salmon roe and lemon juice over the turnips. Serve them on a plate edged with chrysanthemum leaves.

Broiled and Sautéed Foods

Teriyaki Beef Rolls

(4 servings)

INGREDIENTS

4 slices tender beef about 3
  inches wide and $\frac{1}{2}$ inch thick
4 sections burdock same length
  as beef slices

3 tbsp salad oil
1 lemon
4 sections green onions same
  length as beef slices

SAUCE

$\frac{1}{2}$ cup mirin (see p. 201)
$\frac{1}{2}$ cup soy sauce
5 tbsp sugar

$\frac{1}{2}$ cup light stock
dash monosodium glutamate
1 tbsp vinegar

PREPARATION

1. Peel and scrape burdock; soak for about ten minutes in water to
which has been added about 1 tbsp vinegar. After soaking, put the vinegar solution and the burdock in a saucepan, bring to a boil, and simmer
for 2 or 3 minutes to remove the astringency of the burdock.

2. Place one section of green onion and one section of burdock on
each slice of beef. Roll firmly and tie with string.

3. Heat salad oil in frying pan and sauté the beef rolls.

4. Combine sauce ingredients, add them to the frying pan, and simmer the meat rolls until done.

5. Remove from heat, drain, and cool. After removing the strings,
cut the rolls into $\frac{1}{2}$-inch lengths. Arrange on a serving dish with a garnish of thin lemon slices.

Mackerel Bean-paste Teriyaki

(4 servings)

INGREDIENTS

1 (1½ lb) whole fresh mackerel, pompano, or sardine cleaned, head and tail removed
⅔ cup white bean paste
1 tbsp fresh ginger root grated
3 tbsp sugar
3 tbsp sake or dry sherry
3 tbsp oil

2 green onions cut in 3-inch lengths
grated rind of 1 lemon
8 ginger sprouts
4 tbsp rice vinegar
2 tbsp sugar
dash monosodium glutamate
cornstarch

PREPARATION

1. Wash fish in cold water and pat dry with paper towels. Carefully remove bones and cut flesh into 3-inch pieces.

2. Thoroughly combine bean paste, grated ginger, sugar, and sake.

3. Coat fish in the bean-paste mixture, cover, and allow to stand refrigerated overnight.

4. Scrape bean-paste mixture from the fish and dust it inside and outside with cornstarch. Reserve bean-paste marinade.

5. Heat oil in a large skillet. Sauté the fish pieces on one side till golden brown, turn, and sauté on the other side. Cover and cook until the fish flakes easily with a fork.

6. After cleaning the ginger sprouts, marinate them for 10 minutes in a mixture of 4 tbsp rice vinegar, 2 tbsp sugar, 4 tbsp water, and dash of monosodium glutamate.

7. In a saucepan combine grated lemon rind and reserved bean-paste marinade. Bring almost to a boil over moderate heat, reduce heat to low, and, stirring constantly, cook till thick. Coat cooked fish with about half the bean paste. In the remaining paste, quickly heat green onion sections. These and the ginger sprouts are served as a garnish with the fish.

Pork Rolls

(4 servings)

INGREDIENTS

4 thin slices lean pork about
   3 inches wide
1 stalk of burdock cut into 4
   sections same length as pork

2 tbsp vinegar
1 cup light stock
flour for dredging
dash pepper (preferably sansho
   pepper; see p. 213)

SEASONINGS A

1 tbsp soy sauce

2 tbsp sugar

SEASONINGS B

3 tbsp soy sauce
3 tbsp sake

3 tsp sugar
1 tsp grated ginger root

SEASONINGS C

1 tbsp mirin or sweet sherry
½ tsp monosodium glutamate

1 tbsp cornstarch
½ cup water

PREPARATION

1. Peel and scrape burdock. Cut each section into quarters vertically. Soak in about 5 cups of water to which have been added 2 tbsp vinegar. Drain. Boil burdock in light stock for about 2 or 3 minutes; add seasonings A and remove from heat.

2. Combine seasonings B in a bowl; add the pork and marinate for 30 minutes.

3. Remove pork slices and dredge well in flour. Reserve the marinade. Put four thin slices of burdock in the center of each slice of pork. Roll tightly and tie with string.

4. Bring the reserved marinade to a boil and add seasonings C.

5. Coat each roll well with the resulting thickened sauce and broil over charcoal or in a broiler. During the broiling, turn several times and baste with additional sauce. Place on a serving plate and sprinkle the rolls with sansho pepper. Remove the strings and cut each roll into ½-inch lengths.

Ginger Pork

(4 servings)

INGREDIENTS

1 lb pork loin sliced thin	1 tbsp oil
1 tbsp grated ginger root	1 cup soy sauce
2 tbsp sake	4 tbsp sugar

PREPARATION

1. Combine soy sauce, sake, and sugar in saucepan; bring to a boil. Remove from heat and add ginger juice. Marinate pork slices in this mixture for 30 minutes.

2. In a heavy skillet heat 1 tbsp oil. Sauté the pork slices. Turn them once as soon as the meat changes color. Serve immediately.

Chicken Rolls

(4 servings)

INGREDIENTS

2 boned chicken legs	1 tbsp sugar
6 sections green onion cut to same length as chicken meat	$\frac{1}{2}$ cup water
	$\frac{1}{2}$ tbsp cornstarch
3 tbsp soy sauce	dash pepper (preferably sansho
3 tbsp mirin (see p. 201)	pepper; see p. 213)
$\frac{1}{2}$ tsp monosodium glutamate	

PREPARATION

1. Lightly pound chicken meat with back of a butcher knife or wooden mallet. Place three sections of green onion in the center of each piece of chicken meat. Roll tightly and secure with string.

2. Prepare basting sauce by combining and bringing to a boil soy sauce, mirin, monosodium glutamate, sugar, water, and cornstarch. Broil the chicken rolls in a thoroughly preheated broiler. Basting as needed with the sauce, continue to broil until the rolls are done. Remove from broiler and cool. Remove strings and cut rolls into $\frac{1}{2}$-inch lengths. Sprinkle the rolls with sansho pepper. An excellent garnish for these rolls is about $\frac{1}{2}$ can of gingko nuts salted lightly and broiled.

Skewered Chicken Barbecue

(4 servings)

INGREDIENTS

boned meat from 1 frying chicken
  or from 3 large chicken legs
½ cup soy sauce
½ cup mirin (see p. 201)
2 tbsp sugar
½ tsp monosodium glutamate
1 cup water
1 tbsp cornstarch dissolved in
  water

2 tbsp pepper (preferably
  sansho pepper; see p. 213)
½ daikon radish grated fine
6 green onions cut into ½-inch
  lengths
2 quartered green peppers
6 halved mushrooms

PREPARATION

1. Cut the chicken meat into bite-size pieces.

2. Prepare basting sauce by combining and bringing to a boil mirin, soy sauce, sugar, water, and monosodium glutamate. When this mixture boils, add cornstarch. Simmer 1 or 2 minutes and remove from heat.

3. Arrange chicken meat, onions, green peppers, and mushrooms in alternation on bamboo skewers.

4. Thoroughly preheat broiler. First lightly broil the skewered meat and vegetables. Then baste well with sauce and continue broiling until they are done. It will be necessary to baste them 4 or 5 times. Do not overcook, for the vegetables will dry out and the chicken will toughen.

5. Sprinkle the skewered foods with pepper and serve them with a garnish of grated daikon radish.

Chicken Patty

(4 servings)

INGREDIENTS

1 lb ground chicken
1 egg
2 tbsp bean paste
1 tsp white sesame seeds
3 tbsp sugar

salad oil
2 tbsp all-purpose flour
dash monosodium glutamate
additional sesame seeds for
  garnish

PREPARATION

1. In a saucepan over a moderate heat combine sugar and bean paste. Cook until the mixture is thick and thoroughly blended. Cool.

2. Combine this paste with the ground chicken. Add the lightly beaten egg, flour, monosodium glutamate, and sesame seeds. Blend well.

3. Spread this mixture evenly in a greased baking pan. Sprinkle the top with additional seeds. Bake in a moderate oven (350°) for approximately 15 minutes. Cool and cut into bite-size pieces. This patty may also be sautéed in a heavy skillet.

Fragrant Fried Chicken

(5 servings)

INGREDIENTS
about 1 lb boned chicken meat
MARINADE

1½ tbsp finely grated ginger root	2 tbsp sugar
½ cup soy sauce	½ tbsp cornstarch
½ cup mirin (see p. 201)	½ cup water
½ tsp monosodium glutamate	1 tbsp oil

PREPARATION

1. Cut chicken into bite-size pieces and marinate in combined marinade ingredients for from 2 to 3 hours for best flavor.

2. Heat salad oil in a heavy skillet and sauté chicken till done. Add some of the marinade to the pan if necessary but be careful to use only moderate heat because soy sauce scorches easily.

Bonito Teriyaki with Sesame Seeds

(4 servings)

INGREDIENTS

4 fresh bonito steaks (or salmon steaks)	3 tbsp soy sauce
2 tbsp white sesame seeds	2 tbsp sugar
1 tbsp bean paste	1 tbsp grated fresh ginger root
2 tbsp mirin (see p. 201)	1 tbsp salt

1. Sprinkle bonito steaks with salt.

2. Parch sesame seeds over a low heat and crush. Mix these with bean paste, mirin, soy sauce, sugar, and ginger. Marinate bonito steaks in this sauce for 1 hour. Remove and drain briefly. Reserve marinade.

3. Broil bonito under medium heat until brown, turning once and basting with marinade two or three times during cooking.

Green Pepper and Eggplant Basted in Bean Paste

(4 servings)

INGREDIENTS

4 green peppers
4 small eggplants
sesame oil for frying

2 or 3 tbsp parched white
    sesame seeds

SAUCE

6 tbsp white bean paste mixed
    with 3 tbsp water
3 tbsp sake

3 tbsp sugar
$\frac{1}{2}$ tsp monosodium glutamate

PREPARATION

1. Wash and cut eggplants into $\frac{1}{2}$-inch slices. Wash green peppers; discard seeds, and cut the peppers into quarters.

2. In a sauce pan over a low heat combine bean paste and water mixture with sake, sugar, and monosodium glutamate. Cook gently until the ingredients are thoroughly blended.

3. The eggplant and green peppers may be cooked in either of the following ways. They may be coated with sesame oil and broiled and then after being coated with the bean-paste sauce return to the broiler for a few minutes. Or they may be fried first in sesame oil, coated with bean paste, and returned to the frying pan for finishing. Garnish with sesame seeds.

Fried Foods

Deep-fried Shrimp in Noodles

INGREDIENTS

1 lb shelled shrimp
1 package harusame (or
vermicelli)
¼ cup cornstarch
monosodium glutamate and salt

1 cup tempura batter made
according to directions on
p. 86
1 egg
oil for frying

PREPARATION

1. Devein shrimp and chop harusame into about ⅛-inch lengths.
2. Beat the egg.
3. Dip the shrimp into cornstarch, then into egg, and finally into batter. Dip the coated shrimp into chopped harusame. In a deep skillet heat more then 1 inch of cooking oil. Slip the coated shrimp into the deep fat and fry till golden. Serve with mixed monosodium glutamate and salt.

Mixed Fritters

INGREDIENTS

2 slices of ham chopped or one
can crab meat
1 stalk burdock
1 lotus root
½ bunch trefoil or watercress

1 sweet potato
1 package harusame
1 cup tempura batter (see p. 86)
oil for frying

PREPARATION

1. Peel and julienne cut lotus root, sweet potato, and burdock.
2. Soak burdock in a weak vinegar-water solution for about 10 minutes.
3. Chop harusame into 1-inch lengths. If using crab, carefully remove all bonelike membranes. Reserve the largest pieces for garnish.
4. Drain all vegetables, mix together with ham (or crab), and add

enough tempura batter to form a cohesive mixture.

5. In a deep skillet heat cooking oil. Gently drop the batter and vegetable mixture, one tablespoon at a time, into the hot oil and fry till golden. The fritters require longer to fry than shrimp tempura. Serve with tempura dip (see p. 87) and grated daikon radish.

Tempura

INGREDIENTS

1 1b combination of prawns, shrimp, white-flesh fish

½ 1b combination of asparagus, eggplant, green pepper, potatoes, sweet potatoes, fresh mushrooms, or any other fresh vegetables in season

BATTER 1

1 cup flour

1 cup water

1 egg yolk

½ tsp sake or rice vinegar

BATTER 2 (crispier than Batter 1)

1 cup flour

½ cup cornstarch

dash salt

¼ tsp monosodium glutamate

1 egg

1 tsp baking powder

1½ cups water

BATTER 3 (green in color)

1 cup flour

1 cup water

1 egg

2 tsp powdered green tea

SAUCE

1 cup stock No. 1 (p. 69)

1 tsp sugar

2 tbsp soy sauce

grated daikon radish or fresh ginger root

¼ cup sake or dry sherry

½ tsp monosodium glutamate

PREPARATION

To prepare any of the three batters, first combine the dry ingredients, then beat the egg separately and add it to the water. Finally, combine the liquid mixture with the dry ingredients and mix quickly and lightly. Do not worry about lumps.

Shell and devein the shrimp. All fish must be filleted and cut in moderately small pieces. To make butterfly shrimps, slit them down the back and flatten them lightly with the side of a kitchen knife before coating them in batter. Lightly salt all ingredients. You may make two or three transverse gashes in each shrimp to prevent it from curling during frying.

Clean, peel, and cut into bite-size pieces all the vegetables you intend to use. Arrange all ingredients on platters ready for frying. Have the batter ready. Prepare dip sauce by combining and heating the sauce ingredients. Serve the sauce in individual bowls large enough to accommodate the largest tempura pieces.

In a deep skillet, heat at least 3 cups of oil to 370 degrees. Be generous with the oil and always add fresh oil before cooking a new batch of tempura. Dip each of the fish, shrimp, and vegetable ingredients in batter, lower a few pieces into the hot oil, and fry till golden and light. Remove, drain quickly, and serve at once with the sauce and some grated daikon radish or grated fresh ginger root.

Shrimp Balls

(4 servings)

INGREDIENTS

1 lb shrimp or prawns
1 egg separated
¼ tsp salt
dash monosodium glutamate
1½ tbsp cornstarch

2 packages raw fine wheat
    noodles (somen) (see noodles;
    p. 202)
oil for frying
grated fresh ginger root and
    daikon radish for garnish

PREPARATION

1. Shell and devein the shrimp. Mince shrimp and combine with 1 beaten egg yolk, ¼ tsp salt, and dash of monosodium glutamate. Reserve the egg white and beat it lightly. Shape this mixture into 12 balls, and roll them in cornstarch.

2. Cut the raw noodles into ½-inch lengths. Dip the shrimp balls first into the egg white and then into the chopped noodles.

3. In a deep skillet heat about three cups of oil to 370 degrees. Gently lower the coated shrimp balls into the oil and fry until the balls float to the surface. Drain and serve with tempura sauce (see p. 86) to which have been added grated ginger root and daikon radish.

Braised Dishes

Beef Braised in Grated Radish

(4 servings)

INGREDIENTS

1 lb beef

10 green onions

1 cup grated daikon radish

$\frac{1}{4}$ cup soy sauce

3 tbsp oil

dash monosodium glutamate

PREPARATION

1. To slice meat very thin freeze it slightly; it can then be shaved paper thin.

2. Cut green onions into 1-inch slices.

3. Grate daikon and drain.

4. Heat skillet and add 3 tbsp oil. Put one-third of thinly sliced meat in hot skillet. Add green onions and grated daikon. Sauté this mixture briefly. Add soy sauce and monosodium glutamate. Simmer till done, adding more soy sauce if necessary. Serve with rice and pickled vegetables.

Beef in Bean-paste Sauce

(4 servings)

INGREDIENTS

1 lb beef thinly sliced

2 onions chopped

5 tbsp red bean paste

2 small pieces minced ginger root

$\frac{1}{2}$ cup sake

3 tbsp sugar

PREPARATION

1. Put the meat into a large saucepan, add onion, ginger and sake; bring to a boil.

2. When meat is heated, combine 3 tbsp sugar and 5 tbsp red bean paste. Simmer until meat is done and well coated with sauce. This takes only a few minutes.

Chinese-cabbage Rolls

(4 servings)

INGREDIENTS

1 head Chinese cabbage
1 lb ground pork
½ onion
2 bouillon cubes
1 egg
1 tsp salt

pepper
kampyo (see p. 200)
2 tbsp cornstarch
2 tsp soy sauce
½ tbsp sugar
monosodium glutamate

PREPARATION

1. Parboil Chinese cabbage. Reserve water. Separate leaves without breaking and drain them on a towel.

2. Chop onion and mix well with ground pork, egg, 1 tsp salt, and pepper.

3. Place some meat mixture on each cabbage leaf. Roll and tie with kampyo.

4. Place rolls in pan and cover with cabbage water. Add bouillon cubes and simmer 20 minutes. Remove cabbage rolls. Dissolve 2 tbsp cornstarch in water and add soy sauce, sugar, and monosodium glutamate. Heat till thick and clear. Pour sauce over cabbage rolls and serve.

Chicken Curry

(4 servings)

INGREDIENTS

1 chicken (2–3 lbs)
½ cup chopped onion
5 tbsp butter or oil
2½ tbsp curry powder
1 tsp salt
1 tsp minced garlic
2 cups chicken broth
2 cups fresh coconut milk

6 tbsp flour
½ cup sliced mushrooms
½ ginger root grated
1 carrot
2 potatoes
2-3 bay or celery leaves
2 tbsp steak sauce
2 tbsp ketchup

PREPARATION

1. Clean chicken and cut into serving pieces.

2. Peel potatoes and carrots and cut into coarse dice.

3. Marinate chicken in grated ginger for 15 minutes.

4. Sauté onion and garlic in 3 tbsp butter over medium heat until onion is golden. Add flour and curry powder; sauté well. Add chicken broth and salt.

5. In a separate skillet sauté chicken in 2 tbsp butter; add potatoes, carrots, and mushrooms. Then add coconut milk.

6. Combine chicken, potatoes, carrots, and mushrooms with mixture from step 4. Add bay or celery leaves and simmer till all ingredients are done. Remove bay or celery leaves. Add 2 tbsp ketchup and 2 tbsp steak sauce.

7. Serve with rice, chopped pickled onions, and chopped pickled ginger.

One-pot Cookery

Pork and Spinach Casserole

(4 servings)

INGREDIENTS

1 lb pork roast
1 bunch spinach
5-inch strip kelp
1 tsp salt
1 small clove garlic
1 2-inch section fresh ginger root

1 lemon
$\frac{1}{2}$ cup chopped green onions
1 cup grated daikon radish
    flavored with soy sauce and
    red pepper

PREPARATION

1. Slice the pork very thin against the grain. Wash spinach and cut into 2-inch lengths. Peel ginger and garlic; slice very thin. Slice lemon.

2. Put kelp in the bottom of a deep crockery casserole; fill the casserole with water. Add salt and bring the mixture to a boil. Add garlic and ginger. Next add the meat and spinach a little at a time. Simmer until the ingredients are tender. Serve in the casserole. Lemon slices, chopped green onion, and flavored grated daikon radish are used as garnishes.

Chinese-cabbage Casserole

(4 or 5 servings)

INGREDIENTS

1 small head (about 2 lbs)
   Chinese cabbage
1 package harusame (or
   vermicelli)
½ kamaboko fish loaf (see p. 200)
10 large shiitake mushrooms,
   dried or fresh

5 fillets of white-flesh fish
2 chicken legs
5 cups stock No. 2 (see p. 69)
3 stalks spinach
1 tbsp light soy sauce
2 tbsp mirin (see p. 201)
1 tsp salt

PREPARATION

1. Parboil spinach; drain. Parboil Chinese cabbage, drain, separate leaves, and lightly crush the hard base sections with the back of a knife. Spread cabbage leaves on a flat surface for rolling. (This step is easier if you own a Japanese-style bamboo mat created for this purpose.) Spread the spinach leaves on top of the cabbage and roll tightly. Cut the rolls into 1½-inch lengths.

2. Soften the harusame in boiling water. Drain and cut into convenient lengths. Slice the fish loaf. Clean the mushrooms and remove and discard stems. Dried mushrooms must be softened in lukewarm water. Bone chicken legs and cut meat into bite-size pieces. Arrange the prepared ingredients on a large serving platter.

3. Arrange some of the cabbage roll slices in the center of the bottom of a deep crockery casserole. Around them arrange the chicken, harusame, fish loaf, fish, and mushrooms. Pour stock over them and bring to a boil. Season with soy sauce, mirin, and salt. Lower the heat and simmer for 2 to 3 minutes. Guests may begin eating from the casserole as soon as the chicken is done. Replenish ingredients as needed.

Chicken and Vegetable Casserole

(4 or 5 servings)

INGREDIENTS

4 boned chicken legs
1 daikon radish
1 or 2 carrots

8 fresh mushrooms
4 green onions minced
8 cups water

1 tbsp salt
1 cake bean curd
1 medium head Chinese cabbage

1 bunch edible chrysanthemum
   leaves

VINEGAR AND SOY-SAUCE DIP
1 tbsp mirin (see p. 201)
6 tbsp soy sauce
4 tbsp vinegar

1 green onion
red pepper

PREPARATION

1. Peel, slice, and cut into flower shapes the radish and carrots. Parboil until just tender. After removing from heat, plunge into cold water; drain. If the mushrooms are large, slice them. Cut the green onions into 1½-inch lengths. Cut bean curd in small cubes.

2. Cut the chicken meat into bite-size pieces. Wash thoroughly under cold water. Put chicken into a saucepan, cover with cold water, and bring to a boil. Remove scum from surface of water and degrease the broth. Simmer over a low heat for from 30 to 40 minutes. Salt lightly. Remove chicken, but reserve broth.

3. Combine mirin, soy sauce, and vinegar in a saucepan and heat to the boiling point. After seasoning with red pepper and minced green onion, use this mixture as a dip for the chicken and vegetables.

4. Arrange chicken meat, bean curd, and vegetables on a plate. Fill a deep crockery casserole with the broth from step 2. Bring to a boil at the table, add prepared ingredients, and permit guests to serve themselves from the casserole. They should coat pieces of meat and vegetables in the dip before eating.

Sea Bream and Vegetable Casserole

(4 or 5 servings)

INGREDIENTS

1 whole sea bream or other
   white-flesh fish (about 3½ lbs)
2 oz harusame (or vermicelli)
1 bunch edible chrysanthemum
   leaves
1 medium head Chinese cabbage
5 mushrooms

½ bunch spinach
1½ cakes bean curd
4 green onions
1 6-inch square of kelp
5 tbsp vinegar
3 tbsp soy sauce

½ tsp monosodium glutamate   6 cups water
2 tbsp stock No. 1 (p. 69)   2 tbsp mirin (see p. 201)

PREPARATION

1. Clean and fillet the fish. Slice the meat into 1-inch slices. After cutting into large chunks, grill the head and spine of the fish over a high heat.

2. Cut the green onion into 1½-inch diagonal slices. After washing the mushrooms, remove and discard the stems and cut an ornamental cross design in the tops. Cut bean curd into 1-inch cubes. Steam Chinese cabbage until barely tender in 1 cup boiling water in a tightly covered pan. Drain, sprinkle with salt, and cool. Thoroughly clean the spinach and wilt it in ½ cup water. When it is barely tender but has not lost its color, remove from the heat, rinse in cold water, straighten the leaves, and allow them to drain. Spread the steamed cabbage flat. Place the drained spinach in the center of the cabbage and roll carefully. Cut the roll into 1-inch slices. Wash the chrysanthemum leaves and discard the roots. Separate into sprigs. Soak harusame in lukewarm water for from 5 to 6 minutes; cut into 2½-inch lengths. Arrange all the ingredients decoratively on a large platter.

3. Wipe both sides of the kombu with a damp cloth. Put it into a deep pot about ⅔ full of cold water. Bring this not quite to the boiling point over a medium heat. Add mirin, fish head and bones, and sliced fish. Simmer gently, taking care to skim off all scum that surfaces. Add bean curd, green onion, chrysanthemum leaves, mushrooms, cabbage-spinach rolls, and harusame. Simmer, once again taking care to skim off scum.

4. Prepare a dip by mixing vinegar, soy sauce, monosodium glutamate, and stock. An attractive additional dip or garnish can be made by heaping julienne green onions on one small plate and finely grated daikon radish tinted with soy sauce on another.

5. Serve the broth, fish, and vegetables in the cooking pot. Do not overcook; these ingredients are at their best when just done. Guests may serve themselves, dipping individual morsels in the soy-sauce and vinegar dip.

Oyster Casserole

(4 servings)

INGREDIENTS

1 qt husked large oysters
2 green onions
2 pieces of green fu (wheat
gluten cake; see p. 198)
4 dried shiitake mushrooms
1 bunch watercress
1 carrot
vinegar

2 tbsp red bean paste
9 tbsp white bean paste
3 tbsp mirin (see p. 201)
mixture of 8 tbsp sake and
dash monosodium glutamate
mixture of 4 cups water with
$\frac{1}{4}$ tsp monosodium glutamate
1 lemon

PREPARATION

1. Remove sand, grit, and bits of shell from the oysters by washing them well in lightly salted water. Pour hot water over them, allow them to stand for a few seconds, then drain.

2. Cut green onions into diagonal slices. Soften fu in water then squeeze out as much moisture as possible. Cut it into 1-inch slices.

3. Peel, slice, and cut carrot into flower shapes. Slice lemon and cut it into attractive shapes. Tenderize the dried mushrooms by soaking them in lukewarm water. Remove and discard stems. Cut watercress into $1\frac{1}{2}$-inch lengths.

4. Mix red and white bean paste with mirin and mixture of 8 tbsp sake and 1 dash monosodium glutamate. Blend thoroughly and heat briefly over medium heat. Using a rubber spatula, spread this bean-paste mixture evenly around the sides of a deep crockery casserole. After putting the casserole on a low heat, pour in 4 cups of water to which has been added $\frac{1}{4}$ tsp monosodium glutamate. Add oysters, onions, watercress, mushrooms, and fu. Simmer until the oysters are just done serve at once.

Tuna and Green-onion Casserole

(4 servings)

INGREDIENTS

1 lb fresh boned tuna
6 or 7 green onions

2 cakes lightly toasted bean
curd
1 can shirataki (see p. 205)

3 cups stock No. 1 (see p. 69)
⅔ cup soy sauce
6 tbsp mirin (see p. 201)
2 tsp sugar
dash monosodium glutamate

dash hot pepper (preferably
    shichimi togarashi; see pepper;
    p. 202)
dash Japanese pepper
4 eggs (1 for each guest)

PREPARATION

1. Cut the tuna into chunks about 1½ by 1 by ½ inch. Cut the green onions into thick diagonal slices. Cut the bean curd into 1-inch cubes. Cut the shirataki into 2-inch lengths and parboil.

2. Make sauce by pouring the mirin into a heavy skillet and bringing it to a boil. Ignite it and when the alcohol has burned off, remove skillet from heat. Add stock, soy sauce, sugar, and monosodium glutamate. Return to stove and heat gently for a few minutes.

3. Pour the happojiru sauce into a bowl or pitcher and arrange the fish, onions, and shirataki on a large platter.

4. The next step is done at the table. Some heat source—like an electric skillet—is needed. In the bottom of the skillet make an even layer of green onions. Cover this with an even layer of shirataki, and top these ingredients with the tuna chunks. Pour the happojiru sauce over these ingredients and allow it to boil. When the tuna has changed color, turn it over and cook the other side. Add the bean curd, cook for 1 or 2 minutes more, and invite the guests to serve themselves.

5. Prepare a small individual bowl of dip for each guest by breaking a raw egg into it, beating it lightly, and sprinkling it with hot pepper and Japanese pepper.

Clam Casserole

(4 servings)

INGREDIENTS

1 qt shelled clams
1 pint blood clams
1 cake bean curd
1 bunch watercress
2 green onions

4 large leaves Chinese cabbage
4 cups stock No. 1 (p. 69)
5 tbsp sake
2 tbsp soy sauce

1 tsp salt	1 green onion chopped for
1 lemon	garnish

PREPARATION

1. Wash clams and blood clams in salted water. Drain. Cut bean curd into ½-inch cubes. Cut watercress into 1-inch lengths. Cut green onions into diagonal slices. Parboil separately Chinese cabbage and watercress. Roll the cress inside the cabbage leaves and slice the rolls into 1-inch lengths.

2. To stock made by briefly boiling a 6-inch piece of kelp in water add sake, soy sauce, and salt. Bring to a boil. Gradually add the onions, clams and blood clams, and bean curd. Finally add the cabbage rolls.

3. Serve with a garnish of chopped green onion and lemon wedges.

Fowl Served in Sea Shells

(4 servings)

INGREDIENTS

1 Cornish game hen or wild duck quartered	4 large abalone shells
1 daikon radish	1 tbsp chicken fat
1 green onions	5 tbsp soy sauce
1 bunch parsley	2 tbsp mirin (see p. 201)
4 8-inch strips of kampyo (see p. 200)	2 tbsp sake
	5 tbsp stock No. 1 (p. 69)

PREPARATION

1. Wash the abalone shells and plug the holes with sections of kampyo.

2. Combine the soy sauce, mirin, sake, and stock. Heat this sauce and add the chicken fat to it. Add sugar and extra soy sauce if needed: the sauce should be slightly salty.

3. Peel the daikon radish and cut it into 1½-inch sections. Cut the onions into similar sections. Divide the sauce among the four shells; add the daikon and onion. Putting the shells directly over the source of heat, cook the vegetables in the sauce till they are about half done.

4. Add the hen breast first, then legs. Simmer for a few minutes

then turn the hen to ensure an even coating of sauce. Continue to cook until the hen is done.

5. Serve in the shells placed on serving dishes. Garnish with parsley.

Simmered Bean Curd

(4 or 5 servings)

INGREDIENTS

2 to 4 cakes bean curd
1 qt oysters
1 bunch spinach
½ bunch trefoil or watercress
1 4-inch strip kelp
5 green onions

1 cup shaved dried bonito
   (katsuobushi, see p. 200)
1 2-inch section fresh ginger root
1 sheet dried laver (nori)
sake

SEASONINGS A

1 cup soy sauce
2 tbsp mirin (see p. 201)

1 tbsp stock
dash monosodium glutamate

PREPARATION

1. Cut the bean cake into large pieces.
2. Wash oysters in salted water, drain, and sprinkle with sake.
3. Wash spinach, trefoil, and green onions. Cut them all into 1½-inch lengths.
4. Prepare dips and garnishes. Finely chop 1 green onion, plunge into cold water, drain, and put in a small serving bowl. Combine seasonings A in a saucepan. Bring to a boil. Remove from heat and dilute with water to taste. Put in a serving bowl. Cut the laver into 1½-inch lengths and put in a serving dish. Grate the ginger and put it in a small serving bowl.
5. Put the kelp in the bottom of a deep crockery casserole. Cover with cold water and bring to a boil. Lower the heat. Add prepared ingredients and cook till just done. Guests may serve themselves. Each person should have his own small dip bowl into which he may put sauce garnished to taste with onions, ginger, shaved dried bonito, and laver.

Cuttlefish Casserole

(4 servings)

INGREDIENTS

1 cuttlefish
1 head Chinese cabbage
8 mushrooms
1 stalk broccoli
1 carrot
2 green onions
1⅓ cup chicken stock
1 tsp sugar

1 tbsp cornstarch
⅓ tsp salt
1 tsp vinegar
3 tbsp oil
stock
dash pepper
dash monosodium glutamate

PREPARATION

1. Cut 1 green onion into 1½-inch lengths. Halve these lengthwise. Chop the other green onion for garnish.

2. Cut Chinese cabbage into slices about 1½ inches thick. Scrape carrot and cut it into short sections; slice these lengthwise. Clean mushrooms, and discard stems. Wash broccoli. Parboil in lightly salted water. Rinse in cold water. Separate broccoli into equal sprigs.

3. Skin cuttlefish. If this proves difficult, it is helpful to rub the cuttlefish thoroughly with a wet cloth. Score the flesh lengthwise then cut into slices about ½ by 1½ inches.

4. Heat 3 tbsp oil in a skillet. Lightly sauté the vegetables and the cuttlefish. Add stock, salt, pepper, sugar, monosodium glutamate, and vinegar. Bring the mixture to a boil. Mix the cornstarch with water; add it to the mixture in the skillet and continue cooking until the sauce thickens.

Eight-treasure Casserole

(4 servings)

INGREDIENTS

4 fillets (about 10 oz) of sea
   bream or yellowtail
4 prawns
4 large clams
12 oysters

4 boned chicken breasts
4 large fresh mushrooms
4 taro roots
12 gingko nuts

⅓ cup vinegar
½ cup soy sauce
pine needles

rock salt
clean pebbles
1 tbsp grated fresh ginger root.

PREPARATION

1. Make decorative scorings on the skin side of the fillets; sprinkle each with salt.
2. Wash and devein prawns.
3. Soak clams in lightly salted water for from 5 to 6 hours. Cut ligaments to prevent clams' opening and losing juices during cooking. Sprinkle salt over the shells.
4. Wash oysters in lightly salted water and sprinkle lightly with salt and sake.
5. Wash the mushrooms. Discard stems and make decorative scorings on the caps.
6. Wash and peal taro roots; boil till tender.
7. Skewer gingko nuts, three to a toothpick.
8. Cut chicken into bite-size pieces. Sprinkle with salt and sake.
9. Cover the bottom of a deep, ovenware casserole with a layer of clean pebbles. Sprinkle the pebbles with rock salt and cover them with a layer of pine needles. Arrange the clams, oysters, sea bream, gingko nuts, chicken breasts, mushrooms, and taro roots attractively on top of the pine needles. Cover the casserole and cook for 10 minutes in a preheated 350-degree oven. Raise heat to 400 degrees and cook for another 7 minutes. Serve in the casserole with a dip sauce made by combining vinegar, soy sauce, and crushed or grated ginger.

Sukiyaki

(4 or 5 servings)

INGREDIENTS

1½ lb sirloin steak sliced into thin 4-inch lengths
2 or 3 large pieces of beef suet
2 medium onions sliced thin
1 or 2 green onions cut in 2-inch lengths

8 large fresh or dried shiitake mushrooms
1 bunch spinach cut in 2-inch lengths
½ cake bean curd cut in 1-inch cubes

1 can shirataki (see p. 205)
1 head Chinese cabbage

1 can bamboo shoots cleaned
and cut in bite-size pieces
5 eggs

SAUCE

½ cup soy sauce
1 cup mirin (see p. 201)

2 tbsp sugar
1 tsp monosodium glutamate

PREPARATION

Combine the sauce ingredients in a pitcher. More sugar or soy sauce
may be added to suit the tastes of the guests.

Arrange prepared meat and vegetables attractively on a large platter.
Sukiyaki, like many Japanese casserole, or nabe, dishes, is cooked at the
table. An electric skillet is convenient for this purpose. Set the skillet at
360 degrees. When it is hot, put the suet in the pan and allow it to melt.
Next add about ⅓ of the meat. Cook it until it changes color then add
about two thirds of the sauce from the pitcher. Turn the meat. Add
some of each of the remaining ingredients and simmer gently for about
10 minutes. Guests may either serve themselves or the hostess may serve
them. In either case, small individual dishes are necessary. In Japan it
is customary to break a raw egg into the serving bowl, beat it lightly
with chopsticks, and dip the cooked meats and vegetables in it before
eating.

Fried Bean Curd and Noodles

(4 servings)

INGREDIENTS

3 bowls of cooked udon noodles
2 hard boiled eggs
4 slices of kamaboko (see p. 200)
½ bunch of spinach

4 pieces fried bean curd (aburaage, see p. 196)
4 small dried mushrooms
5 cups stock No. 1 (p. 69)
dash of monosodium glutamate

SEASONINGS A

3 tbsp sugar
3 tbsp mirin (see p. 201)

3 tbsp soy sauce

SEASONINGS B

2 tbsp salt
½ tbsp sugar

1½ tbsp mirin
1½ tbsp soy sauce

100

PREPARATION

1. Cut aburaage in diagonal slices. Pour hot water on them to remove oil. Add seasonings A. Cover the mixture and cook 5 minutes over medium heat. Set aside. Parboil spinach 30 seconds; plunge it in cold water. Lift it from the water by roots; align leaves and squeeze out water gently. Cut it into 1-inch lengths. Slice the hard-boiled eggs and kamaboko in thin pieces. Soak dried mushrooms in water. When they are soft, combine them with aburaage and seasonings A and cook over medium heat until almost all liquid has evaporated. Remove from heat. Leave in the pan for a while to steep. Remove to a colander to cool.

2. In medium saucepan bring 5 cups stock to a boil. Add seasonings B and a dash of monosodium glutamate.

3. Fill individual bowls with cooked noodles and place an arrangement of dried mushroom, 1 piece of egg, 2 pieces of aburaage, some spinach, and 1 slice of kamaboko fish loaf on each. Garnish the top with finely sliced green onion. Pour over the noodles the soup made in step 2. Serve very hot.

Steamed Foods

Chicken and Shrimp in Egg Custard

(5 servings)

INGREDIENTS

1 chicken breast

5 fresh or frozen shrimps

3 dried shiitake mushrooms

5 half slices of bamboo shoot

5 pieces kamaboko

10 water chestnuts

10 trefoil or watercress leaves

3 eggs

1 tbsp sake

1 tbsp soy sauce

5 slices lemon

salt

SEASONINGS A

2¼ cups water

1½ tsp salt

1 tsp soy sauce

1 tbsp sugar

SEASONINGS B

1 tsp soy sauce

½ tsp sugar

liquid from mushrooms

¼ tsp monosodium glutamate

PREPARATION

1. Slice chicken breast into 5 pieces. Marinate them in soy sauce for from 5 to 6 minutes.

2. Clean and devein shrimp. Shell but leave tails on. Sprinkle with a little salt and 1 tbsp sake.

3. Clean and soak dried mushrooms in water to soften. Cut off and discard stems. Cut tops into quarters. Reserve water.

4. Cut bamboo shoots in fan shapes. Slice water chestnuts and cut into flower shapes.

5. Cook shiitake mushrooms, bamboo-shoots, and water chestnuts in mushroom liquid to which has been added the remainder of seasonings B. Cut trefoil or watercress leaves into 1-inch strips.

6. Combine eggs and seasonings A; beat slowly so that no foam results.

7. Arrange chicken, vegetables, and shrimp in individual heatproof bowls and add egg mixture. Place in the top section of a steamer and

steam for about 15-20 minutes. The custard is done if a metal skewer or knife blade comes out clean after being inserted into it.

Steamed Matsutake Mushrooms

(4 servings)

INGREDIENTS

2 fresh matsutake mushrooms (see p. 201)
4 shrimp
3 chestnuts
12 gingko nuts shelled
8 pieces watercress or trefoil

1 lemon
3 cups stock No. 2 (p. 69)
2 tsp sake
$\frac{2}{3}$ tsp salt
1 tsp soy sauce
monosodium glutamate

PREPARATION

1. Remove stems from matsutake mushrooms and wash well; do not discard. Slice into 8 pieces.
2. Shell and devein shrimp.
3. Shell, hull, and boil the chestnuts.
4. Wash watercress and cut it into $1\frac{1}{2}$-inch pieces.
5. Combine stock, sake, salt, soy sauce, and monosodium glutamate. Put two inches of water in the bottom pan of a steamer. Put the top in place and bring the water to a boil.
6. Put matsutake, gingko nuts, shrimp, and watercress into individual, covered ceramic pots. Add stock. Place pots in steamer. Cover and steam for about 10 minutes.
7. When the broth in the pots reaches the boiling point, remove from steamer. Serve in small dishes with lemon slices.

Sushi

As is true with most good foods, sushi can be made better and more economically at home if one knows a few basic and important things. The following points will help you master the art of making this famous Japanese specialty. Remember to serve it in one of the traditional

Japanese boxes made especially for the purpose or in some attractive serving dish because visual appeal is one of the most important aspects of good sushi.

SUSHI RICE

(a) Never use anything less than top-quality rice.

(b) Wash the rice thoroughly at least three hours before cooking time and allow it to drain in a colander.

(c) Use one cup of water for each cup of rice. Put a strip of kelp (kombu; about 4 by 4 inches) in the water with the rice and allow the mixture to soak in the rice cooker for 30 minutes.

(d) Next remove the kelp, add 2 or 3 tbsp mirin (see p. 201) and cook the rice according to ordinary procedures. When the rice is done, allow it to stand covered for about 7 to 10 minutes before removing it to a large bowl or a wooden rice tub.

(e) Adding the sugar and vinegar. There are two kinds of sushi rice used in two regions of Japan.

In the Kansai—the Osaka and Kyoto area—cooked fish is used in sushi; consequently, the rice base is sweeter.

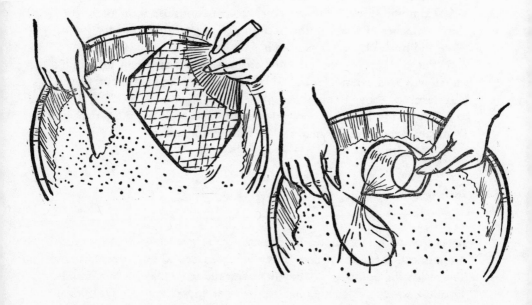

1. Kansai-style Sushi Rice

5 cups rice	1⅔ tsp salt
½ cup vinegar	1 tsp monosodium glutamate
5 tbsp sugar	

In the Kanto area—the Kanto plains including Tokyo—raw-fish sushi is popular, and a less sweet rice is preferred.

2. Kanto-style Sushi Rice

5 cups rice	1⅔ tbsp salt
½ cup vinegar	1 tsp monosodium glutamate
1½ to 3 tbsp sugar	

A second variety of Kanto-style sushi rice is prepared for sushi wrapped in seaweed and stuffed with cucumbers, pickles, or kampyo.

5 cups rice	2 to 3 tsp sugar
½ cup vinegar	dash of salt

All kinds of sushi rice, however, are prepared in the following way. Allow the cooked rice to remain in the cooker for about 15 minutes; remove it to a large bowl. Combine the seasoning ingredients in a small saucepan and heat them. Add them quickly to the rice. Ensure even distribution by using cutting motions through the rice mass with a spatula or a wooden rice server. Cool the rice by either waving a fan over it or training an electric fan on it. In either case, stir the rice constantly until it is cool. This makes the rice shiny and prevents it from becoming mushy.

SUSHI TOPPING INGREDIENTS

1. Kampyo (the meat of a Japanese gourd)

INGREDIENTS
1 package kampyo (see p. 200)
½ cup stock dashi No. 1 (see p. 69)
1 tbsp mirin (see p. 201) ⎫
2 tbsp sake or dry sherry ⎬ for these three you may substitute
2 tbsp sugar ⎭ 3 tbsp sake for a less sweet kampyo
3 tbsp light soy sauce
½ tsp monosodium glutamate

1. Rub salt into the kampyo to soften it quickly. Soak it in lukewarm water till tender. Boil for 10 minutes. Drain it well.

2. Combine and simmer for 10 minutes the stock, kampyo, sugar, sake, mirin, and monosodium glutamate.

3. Add soy sauce and cook for an additional 5 minutes. By this time much of the liquid should have evaporated. Remove the pan from the heat and allow the kampyo to stand in the liquid for a few minutes. Cool in a colander.

2. Mushrooms

INGREDIENTS

8 dried shiitake mushrooms 1 tbsp mirin (see p. 201)
3 tbsp sugar 2 tbsp sake
3 tbsp soy sauce

PREPARATION

1. Soften the mushrooms in lukewarm water. Sprinkle them with a little sugar.

2. Combine all the remaining ingredients, except the soy sauce, in a saucepan. Bring them to a boil and simmer 2 or 3 minutes. Add the mushrooms and simmer for 5 minutes. Add the soy sauce.

3. If you wish the mushrooms to have a gloss, add a few extra drops of mirin at the end of the cooking period.

4. Drain the mushrooms in a colander.

3. Egg Strips

INGREDIENTS

4 eggs 1 tsp salt
4 tsp sugar ½ tsp monosodium glutamate
4 tsp cornstarch 1 tsp oil
3 tbsp water

PREPARATION

1. Beat the eggs very lightly with chopsticks or a fork. Do not allow them to froth.

2. Mix cornstarch and water to a smooth paste; add to the eggs. Add sugar, salt, and monosodium glutamate.

3. Heat oil in a frying pan; then wipe off excess with a paper towel. Cover the bottom of the pan with a thin sheet of the egg mixture much as you might do if you were making crêpes.

Cook briefly on one side; turn. Cook the other briefly and turn the eggs out on a towel or bamboo mat. Allow them to cool then cut into strips about $\frac{1}{4}$ inch wide.

4. Thick Rolled Omelets

INGREDIENTS

2 small white-flesh fish fillets
4 eggs
3 tbsp sugar
1 tbsp mirin (see p. 201)

yellow food coloring
1 tsp salt

PREPARATION

1. Briefly poach fish; squeeze out moisture, and put into a mortar.
2. Break eggs into the same mortar. Add salt, sugar, mirin, and 1 drop food coloring. Pound the mixture to a smooth paste.
3. Oil a heated frying pan. Wipe out excess oil with a paper towel.
4. Cook the egg mixture in thick layers (about $\frac{1}{2}$ inch) slowly until firmly set. Turn out on a bamboo mat (available at Japanese speciality shops) and roll while still warm. Cool before slicing.
Note: This dish may be baked in a slow oven.

5. Sweet-and-sour Lotus Root

INGREDIENTS

1 length fresh lotus root
1 cup vinegar
$1\frac{1}{2}$ tbsp sugar

$\frac{1}{2}$ tsp soy sauce
$\frac{1}{2}$ tsp salt
$\frac{1}{2}$ tsp monosodium glutamate

PREPARATION

1. Peel the lotus root. As you do so, shape it into flower patterns, being careful not to break the divisions among the holes for they are important to the appearance of the cooked root. Soak in a weak vinegar solution for 10 or 15 minutes. Slice crosswise about $\frac{1}{2}$ inch thick. Soak in the vinegar solution an additional 10 or 15 minutes.
2. Bring 3 or 4 cups of water to a boil. Add 1 tsp of vinegar. Plunge the lotus root into the boiling water and remove immediately. Sprinkle with salt and allow it to cool.

3. Combine 1 cup vinegar, 1½ tbsp sugar, ½ tsp soy sauce, and ½ tsp monosodium glutamate in a saucepan. Bring to a boil, add the lotus root, remove from the heat, and allow the root ro marinate in the sauce until needed.

SHELLFISH

Most shellfish are used raw or slightly poached. In Japan akagai, a reddish shellfish called an ark-shell; torigai, cockles; and hamaguri, clams, are popular. All shellfish must stand in fresh water overnight to purge them of grit and sand. After being removed from the shells, the flesh of large shellfish, like the akagai, must be cut longitudinally in half and cleaned. They may then be sprinkled with salt and a few drops of vinegar and kept in a colander or bamboo dish until needed. Rinse before use. Cockles must be salted, washed, sprinkled with boiling water, then rinsed in a weak vinegar-water solution. Clams must be shelled, washed in salted water, sprinkled with salt, sliced, and briefly parboiled.

6. Shrimp

1. Skewer the shrimp before boiling to prevent curling.
2. Bring water to a boil and add a little salt. Drop the skewered shrimp into the water and cook for 3 or 4 minutes. Drain. Remove from skewers. Shell, leaving the tail shells intact. Soak them in a sauce made by combining and heating briefly the following ingredients:

½ cup rice vinegar	½ tsp salt
1½ tbsp sugar	dash monosodium glutamate
½ tsp soy sauce	

7. Fish or Shrimp Flakes

½ lb canned or cooked shrimp or boned fish	½ tsp salt
	dash monosodium glutamate
1 tbsp sugar	red or green food coloring

Mince the shrimp then pound them in a mortar. Add food coloring diluted in water. Combine all ingredients and mix well.

8. Squid

Always use the best fresh squid available. Cut off the legs and skin the squid. Blanch it briefly in boiling water then plunge it immediately into cold water. Slice it according to the requirements of the dish: very fine for certain sushi and in 1-inch lengths for traditional nigirizushi.

9. Fried Bean Curd (Aburaage; see p. 196)

INGREDIENTS

12 cakes fried bean curd	6 tbsp sugar
1½ cups stock No 1 (see p. 69)	½ cup soy sauce
3 tbsp mirin (see p. 201)	dash monosodium glutamate

PREPARATION

1. Parboil the fried bean curd cakes to extract the oil.

2. To the water in the pan add stock, sugar, and mirin, simmer covered over medium heat for 5 or 6 minutes.

3. Add soy sauce and cook until the liquid is reduced to about ⅓ its original volume. Remove from heat. When the bean curd is cool, slice it according to the needs of the recipe.

10. Cucumbers for Kappamaki Rolled Sushi

Wash thoroughly and sprinkle unpeeled cucumbers with salt. Rub them well against chopping board to tenderize the peel. Wash the salt off and slice the cucumber lengthwise into long strips. Prepare a sweet-and-sour sauce by combining the ingredients given below. Pour the sauce over the cucumbers and allow them to marinate until needed.

SWEET-AND-SOUR SAUCE INGREDIENTS

4 tbsp rice vinegar	⅓ tsp salt
1½ tbsp sugar	dash of monosodium glutamate

ROLLED SUSHI

In order to make rolled sushi, a bamboo rolling mat called a makisu is necessary. These are available in many stores specializing in Japanese and oriental products. The rolling method is explained in figures on p. 110. The cutting method is important. First pull the knife toward you as you cut halfway through the roll then push down and away from you as you cut the remainder. Wipe the knife with a damp towel after each cut.

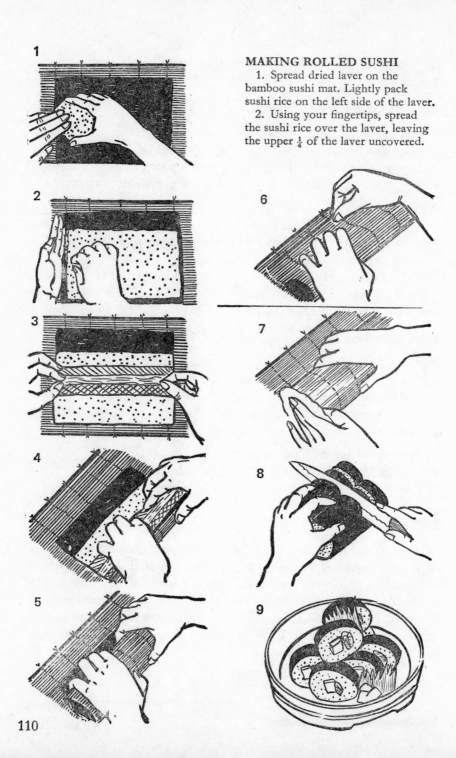

MAKING ROLLED SUSHI

1. Spread dried laver on the bamboo sushi mat. Lightly pack sushi rice on the left side of the laver.

2. Using your fingertips, spread the sushi rice over the laver, leaving the upper $\frac{1}{4}$ of the laver uncovered.

110

3. Place the filling ingredients on the center line of the rice. If you are using ingredients with a high moisture content—for instance shiitake mushrooms—squeeze them well.

4. Putting your thumbs under the forward edge of the bamboo mat and holding the filling ingredients in place with your other fingers, lift the mat as shown.

5. Roll the mat over so that the edge of the layer of rice close to you is aligned with the far edge of the rice. Press lightly as you roll the mat.

6. Holding the upper edge of the bamboo mat with your right hand, and pressing the roll with your left hand, continue to roll the sushi until the uncovered section of laver is on the bottom of the roll.

7. Adjust the shape of the roll and firmly press the ends with a moist towel.

8. Remove the bamboo mat. First cut the rolls in half; then, aligning the halves carefully cut again to make eight sections.

9. The arrangement shown here is attractive: two rows of three pieces, each set in staggered diagonal lines, and two pieces placed on top.

1. Tomoe-pattern Sushi

INGREDIENTS

rice cooked and prepared for sushi
filling of kampyo, eggs prepared according to the recipe on pp. 105, 106.
spinach and mushrooms prepared as described on pp. 101, 106.
sheets of laver for rolling

PREPARATION

1. Spread a sheet of laver on the bamboo mat. Pile the rice on the laver; the layer of rice must be thicker on the part of the laver close to you, must taper off gradually toward the opposite side, and must cover $\frac{3}{4}$ of the sheet of laver.

2. In the center of the rice arrange a straight line of some of the filling ingredients.

3. Roll so as to make a complete turn with $\frac{1}{2}$ the sheet of laver. Cut a strip of laver from a fresh sheet about $\frac{1}{3}$ the width of the full sheet. With this cover the exposed rice. Roll again. Superimpose the rolls so

Cover exposed rice with strip of laver cut
to one-third the width of a full sheet.

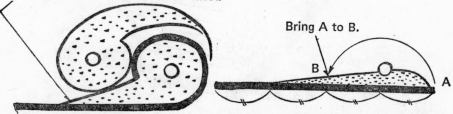

Bring A to B.

that each faces in the opposite direction. Slice. The name of this kind of sushi derives from the commalike shapes resulting from the rolling method. The tomoe—a comma shaped symbol—is often used in decorations, crests, and banners in the Orient.

2. Flower Sushi

INGREDIENTS

rice prepared for sushi

3 sheets of laver

egg strips (see p. 106)

1 cucumber

PREPARATION

1. Over a low flame, lightly toast the fronts and backs of three sheets of laver until they are crisp and dry. Cut two of the sheets vertically into three equal parts for a total of six strips. Coat the strips of laver with sushi rice and place some egg strips in the center of each. Following the procedures for rolled sushi (p. 109), roll each strip of rice-coated laver to make tapering, petal-section units like that shown in Fig. A. There must be six of these.

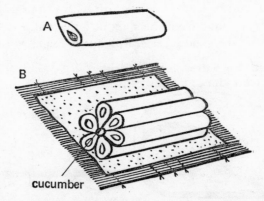

cucumber

2. Spread the remaining piece of laver on a bamboo rolling mat and coat it with thin layer of sushi rice. On top of this place the six rolls arranged to form a flower (Fig. B). A strip of cucumber is used in the center of the flower. Once again following the procedure for rolled sushi, enclose the flower shape in the rice-coated sheet of laver. Cut and arrange on a plate as for rolled sushi.

3. Cucumber Rolls

INGREDIENTS

1 cucumber prepared as described on p. 109 and cut into four lengthwise strips
2 sheets of toasted laver cut in halves

Japanese horseradish (wasabi)
rice prepared for sushi
white sesame seeds

PREPARATION

1. Spread $\frac{1}{2}$ sheet of laver on the bamboo rolling mat. Coat all but about $\frac{1}{4}$ inch along the far edge with an even layer of sushi rice.

2. Spread prepared Japanese horseradish along the center of the rice layer and top this with a strip of cucumber. Sprinkle the rice layer lightly with white sesame seeds. Roll and slice as described on p. 110.

4. Tuna Rolls

INGREDIENTS (4 rolls)

2 sheets of toasted laver cut in halves
4 long slender strips of raw tuna cut to the lengths of the laver sheets.

rice for sushi
Japanese horseradish (wasabi)

PREPARATION

Spread $\frac{1}{2}$ sheet of toasted laver on the rolling mat. Coat all but the far $\frac{1}{4}$ inch of the laver with an even layer of sushi rice. Spread some Japanese horseradish along the center of the rice layer and top this with a strip of raw tuna. Roll and cut as described on p. 110. Traditionally these rolls are cut on diagonal lines.

5. Shinoda Sushi

INGREDIENTS

rice for sushi

2 cakes of fried bean curd (aburaage, p. 196) prepared as described on
   p. 109 and cut as described below

dried mushrooms prepared as described on p. 106

$\frac{1}{3}$ pkg kampyo prepared as described on p. 105 and uncut

$\frac{1}{2}$ bunch parboiled spinach

pickled red ginger (beni shoga; see p. 210) cut julienne style

PREPARATION

1. Fried bean curd cakes are hollow and resemble a bag. Make flat
sheets of them by cutting the three closed sides of the bag. Each cake
yields two flat sheets.

2. Lightly salt the spinach.

3. Spread one sheet of bean curd on the rolling mat. Coat $\frac{3}{4}$ of the
sheet with an even layer of sushi rice. Make a line of mushrooms,
spinach, and pickled ginger on the center of the rice. Roll as for cucumber rolls (p. 113). Finally tie the rolls in 5 places with strips of prepared
kampyo (p. 105) and cut between ties.

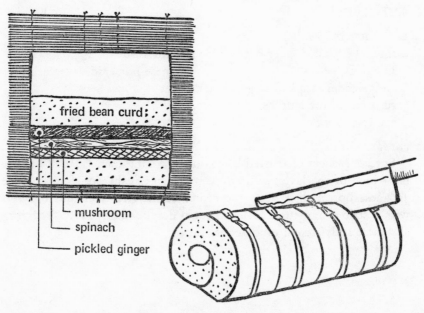

fried bean curd

mushroom
spinach
pickled ginger

6. Inari zushi

(4 servings)

INGREDIENTS

12 cakes fried bean curd
  prepared as described on p.
  109; reserve sauce in which it
  was cooked
⅓ pkg kampyo (p. 200)
rice for sushi (about 4 cups)

white sesame seeds
pickled red ginger sliced thin (p.
  210)
1 stalk burdock
1 carrot

PREPARATION

1. Cut 6 of the prepared aburaage cakes in half; cut the remaining 6 in diagonal slices. This yields 24 small baglike containers into which to stuff the sushi rice.

2. Skin the burdock. Shave it into thin slices. Boil it briefly in a weak vinegar solution to remove astringency. Allow it to cool. Julienne cut the carrot and parboil it.

3. Simmer burdock and carrot in the sauce from the aburaage.

4. Lightly toast the sesame seeds.

5. In a bowl combine the rice with the sesame seeds, carrot, and burdock.

6. Fill the aburaage bags (step 1) with this mixture; tie the rectangular halves with strips of prepared kampyo. Pile the sushi on a plate and garnish with thin slices of pickled red ginger.

Shell-shaped Sushi

(4 servings)

INGREDIENTS

3 cups rice prepared for sushi
4 prepared mushrooms (p. 106)
⅓ pkg prepared kampyo (p. 105)
1 fillet of white-flesh fish
mirin, soy sauce

3 tbsp toasted white sesame
  seeds
4 thin omelets (p. 107; do not
  cut the omelets)

PREPARATION

1. Coarsely chop prepared mushrooms and kampyo.

2. Broil the fish; baste it two or three times with a mixture of one

part mirin to one part soy sauce. Chop the fish.

3. In a large bowl combine sushi rice, chopped mushrooms, kampyo, broiled fish, and toasted white sesame seeds. Mix well.

4. On one half of each of the small omelets, place a generous serving of sushi-rice mixture. Fold the other half over and seal the edges. Heat a skewer in a naked flame and with it press three radiating lines on the top of each stuffed omelet to suggest a seashell.

Sushi Rice Mixed with Vegetables and Seafood

This recipe is for sushi rice served with a sprinkling of a variety of garnishes. The rice is prepared as for any sushi dish, and each of the garnishes is cooked and chopped beforehand. At serving time, heap the rice into attractive individual dishes—bamboo or lacquerware are especially suitable—and sprinkle the garnish ingredients on top.

(4 servings)

INGREDIENTS

4 cups rice prepared for sushi
1 grilled eel or white-flesh
   fish
2 bamboo shoots
2 stalks burdock
4 eggs
5 prawns

4 mushrooms
1 section lotus root (about 4
   inches long)
2 sheets toasted laver
24 kinome pepper leaves (if
   available)

SEASONINGS A

2 tsp mirin (see p. 201)	1 cup stock No. 1
1½ tbsp sugar	dash monosodium glutamate
1½ tbsp light soy sauce	

SEASONINGS B

1½ tbsp sugar	1½ tbsp light soy sauce

SEASONINGS C

4 tsp sugar	½ tsp monosodium glutamate
½ tsp salt	4 tsp cornstarch
3 tbsp stock No. 1 (see p. 69)	

PREPARATION

1. Scrape the burdock, cut it into 1-inch lengths, and divide each of these vertically into four sections. Soak in a weak vinegar solution for about 30 minutes. Boil in vinegar water till tender.

2. Without removing shells, skewer each prawn. Boil for 1 or 2 minutes. Drain, shell, devein, and cut each into four sections. Marinate prawns in a sweet-vinegar sauce (see p. 71).

3. Clean bamboo shoots. Cut them into fan shapes and boil them and cut burdock in seasonings A until tender. Remove vegetables, but reserve liquid.

4. To the liquid from the bamboo shoots and burdock add seasonings B and the mushrooms. Simmer until the mushrooms are tender and have absorbed plenty of the sauce.

5. Peel the lotus root and cut it into flower shapes. Soak in a weak vinegar solution for about 1 minute. Bring this mixture to a boil and simmer gently for a few more minutes. Drain and marinate the lotus root in a sweet-vinegar sauce (see p. 71)

6. Cut the grilled eel or fish fillets into ½-inch pieces.

7. To 4 lightly beaten eggs add seasonings C. Fry this mixture in thin omelets (p. 106). When all of the egg has been cooked, cut the omelet sheets into julienne slices.

8. Julienne cut the laver.

Heap the sushi rice in serving bowls and top with some of each of the garnish ingredients, reserving the egg and laver slices till last.

Five-flavored Sushi

(4 or 5 servings)

INGREDIENTS

4 cups rice prepared for sushi
4 eggs
1 carrot
8 mushrooms
1 4-inch section of lotus root

5 or 6 snow peas
10 cocktail shrimp
1 sheet toasted laver
chopped parsley and julienne-cut
   pickled red ginger for garnish
   (see p. 210)

SEASONINGS A

1 tbsp mirin (see p. 201)
3 tbsp sugar

3 tbsp soy sauce
2 tbsp sake

SEASONINGS B

4 tsp sugar
$\frac{1}{2}$ tsp salt
3 tbsp stock No. 1 (see p. 69)

$\frac{1}{2}$ tsp monosodium glutamate
4 tsp cornstarch

PREPARATION

1. Julienne cut carrot and mushrooms. Simmer till tender in combined seasonings A.

2. Prepare lotus root as described on p. 107.

3. Clean shrimp and boil for 1 or 2 minutes. Combine shrimp, carrot, mushrooms, and lotus root with sushi rice. Mix well.

4. Combine 4 lightly beaten eggs with seasonings B and make thin omelets (p. 106). Cut the omelets julienne style.

5. Parboil snow peas.

6. Heap the rice in individual serving bowls and garnish with egg strips, shrimp, snow peas, laver, parsley, and pickled ginger. This dish is a traditional treat for children's festivals. It is sometimes pressed in molds in the shapes of pine, bamboo, and plum, the plants associated with happy occasions in Japan.

Pressed Sushi

INGREDIENTS

1$\frac{1}{2}$ cups rice prepared for sushi
1 white-flesh fish cut in two
   fillets (tai, or red sea snapper
   is preferred in Japan)

Japanese horseradish (wasabi)
   mixed with water
2 8-inch strips kelp
red pickled ginger (see p. 210)

8 leaves Japanese sansho pepper   kitchen wrap
  (see p. 213)

SWEET-AND-SOUR SAUCE

$\frac{1}{2}$ cup rice vinegar $\frac{1}{2}$ tsp salt
$1\frac{1}{2}$ tbsp sugar   dash monosodium glutamate
$\frac{1}{2}$ tsp soy sauce

PREPARATION

1. After salting the fillets lightly, sandwich them between the pieces of kelp and allow them to stand for at least 1 hour.

2. The fish must be skinned. If the fish dealer has not done this, insert a sharp knife near the tail and, pulling and cutting at the same time, work toward the head till the skin is completely removed. The fillets must then be cut into very thin slices ($\frac{1}{8}$ inch) and into strips about 1 inch wide and 3 inches long.

3. Prepare the sweet-and-sour sauce by combining all the ingredients in a medium bowl. Marinate the fish slices in the sauce for about 30 minutes.

4. Wash the sansho leaves well.

5. Select a wooden or lacquered box about 8 by 3 by 2 inches. After wetting both your hands and the kitchen wrap with a weak vinegar and water solution, line the box carefully with the wrap. In the bottom of the box make an attractive pattern with the marinated fish slices and the Japanese-pepper leaves. On top of this heap the sushi rice. Press it firmly into the box. Next, cover the top with transparent kitchen wrap and continue to press until the rice coheres well. Unmold by pulling gently on the bottom layer of wrap. Cut the sushi into attractive bite-size pieces and serve with a garnish of red pickled ginger cut into julienne strips. To this add a paste made by mixing Japanese horseradish powder and water and allowing it to stand for 5 or 6 minutes to develop full piquancy. Many of the ingredients used in other sushi recipes may be molded this way.

Traditional Sushi-rice Ovals

INGREDIENTS

3 cups rice prepared for sushi
Japanese horseradish (wasabi) mixed to a paste with water.

squid prepared according to direction on p. 108 and sliced about $\frac{1}{4}$-inch thick

raw tuna sliced about $\frac{1}{4}$ inch thick

fillet of small white-flesh fish

shellfish prepared according to directions on p. 108

PREPARATION

1. Some traditional sushi may be made with molds, but it is customary to squeeze it with the bare hands into ovals about 2 inches long and 1 inch wide. To do this, first wet the hands with vineger then, taking a small amount of the rice in one hand, shape it to the correct dimensions and squeeze it firmly from the top with 2 fingers of the other hand.

2. Arrange the topping ingredients on a separate dish. (Note: The fillet of raw white fish must be salted and allowed to stand about 1 hour and then marinated in vinegar for about 30 minutes.) Place the sushi ovals on another dish, and serve the horseradish paste in a separate container. Guests may spread the sushi ovals with a thin coat of horseradish and select the topping they prefer. This is not the procedure followed in Japan, where this kind of food is rarely prepared in the home. Still, served this way, sushi is a delightful and refreshing treat.

Chicken and Mushroom Rice

(4 servings)

INGREDIENTS

3 cups rice

3 cups water

1 boned and skinned chicken breast

1 carrot

2 cakes fried bean curd (aburaage; p. 195)

1 stalk burdock

1 4-inch strip kelp

$\frac{1}{2}$ can shirataki (see p. 205)

2 or 3 shiitake mushrooms

2 green onions

4 tbsp light soy sauce or 3 tbsp dark soy sauce

2 or 3 tbsp mirin (see p. 201)

$\frac{1}{2}$ tsp monosodium glutamate

PREPARATION

1. Wash rice thoroughly and allow it to drain in a colander for 30 minutes.

2. Wash the mushrooms in salt water then slice them thin. Combine mirin, soy sauce, and monosodium glutamate in a small bowl. Marinate the mushrooms in this mixture for 5 minutes. Remove, drain, and set aside.

3. Scrape the burdock. Cut it into thin slices and soak it in a weak vinegar solution to remove astringency. Shred the chicken breast, julienne cut the carrot and fried bean curd. Cut the shirataki in 1-inch lengths. Soak for about 5 minutes in cold water. Slice the onions thin.

4. Combine water, rice, and kelp and allow to stand for 30 minutes. Remove and discard the kelp.

5. Add all the cut ingredients except the mushrooms and onions to the rice pot and bring the mixture to a boil over a medium heat. Lower the heat and add the mushrooms and onions. Cook for about 15 minutes or until all liquid has been absorbed. Remove the pot from the heat and allow it to stand covered for 15 minutes.

Oyster Rice

(4 servings)

INGREDIENTS

3 cups rice
3 cups water
1 4-inch strip kelp
10 oz small oysters
3 green onions
1 grated lemon peel
1 sheet toasted laver
dash monosodium glutamate

1 or 2 sections pickled red ginger cut julienne style (see p. 210)
2 tbsp light soy sauce
2 tbsp mirin (see p. 201)
1 tbsp sake
2 tbsp Japanese horseradish mixed to a paste with water

PREPARATION

1. Wash rice thoroughly and drain it in a colander for 30 minutes.

2. Rinse oysters first in lightly salted water then in fresh cold water. Drain.

3. Cut green onions into $\frac{1}{2}$-inch lengths. Combine onions, oysters, soy sauce, mirin, sake, and monosodium glutamate. Allow these ingredients to marinate for 10 minutes.

4. In a large pot combine water, rice, and kelp; allow this to stand for 30 minutes. Remove and discard the kelp. Strain the marinade

from the oysters and onions and add the liquid to the rice pot. Cover the pot and bring the liquid to a boil. Add oysters and onions; simmer over medium heat for 5 or 6 minutes. Turn the heat to low and continue to cook for 10 minutes. Remove the pot from the heat and allow it to steam covered for 10 minutes.

5. Cut the toasted laver into julienne strips. (Scissors are a convenient tool for this operation.) Mix the rice and oysters well, heap the mixture in serving bowls and top with shredded laver. Serve with garnishes of red pickled ginger and horseradish. This dish is good hot or cold.

Red-bean Rice

(4 servings)

INGREDIENTS

3 cups glutinous rice
1 cup azuki, lentils, or red
    kidney beans
½ tsp salt

2 tbsp mirin (see p. 201)
1 tsp monosodium glutamate
3½ cups stock from cooked
    beans

PREPARATION

1. Wash beans well. Cover with 3 or 4 cups water and bring to a boil. Cover and cook gently over a low heat till done. The bean skins must not break. Skim off scum that forms on the surface.

2. Drain beans and reserve 3½ cups of stock. If there is not enough stock, make up the difference with water.

3. Wash rice well. Soak it in the bean stock for 3 hours.

4. Drain rice, cover it with 3 cups of water, add the beans, salt, mirin, and monosodium glutamate, and simmer over medium heat for from 15 to 20 minutes. Turn heat to low and simmer for another 15 or 20 minutes.

Chestnut Rice

(4 or 5 servings)

INGREDIENTS

2 cups glutinous rice
2 cups plain rice
15 small chestnuts shelled and
    skinned

15 gingko nuts
1½ tsp salt
3 tbsp sake
4 cups water

PREPARATION

1. Soak chestnuts in water for 1 hour.

2. Wash rice thoroughly and allow it to drain in a colander for 30 minutes. In a large pot combine rice and water; allow it to stand for 30 or 40 minutes. Add chestnuts, gingko nuts, salt, and sake.

3. Bring liquid to a boil over a high heat; lower heat and simmer for 20 minutes or until all liquid has been absorbed. Remove from heat and allow to steam covered for 15 minutes.

4. Before serving, mix well to distribute the chestnuts evenly through the rice.

Seafood Rice Bowl

(4 servings)

INGREDIENTS

6 prawns
2 fillets of white-flesh fish
1 carrot (or sweet potato, egg
    plant, green beans, green
    peppers, asparagus)
1 egg yolk beaten in ½ cup ice
    water

1 cup flour
1 cup stock No. 1 (see p. 69)
¼ cup soy sauce
¼ cup mirin (see p. 201)
¼ tsp monosodium glutamate
4 serving bowls filled with
    cooked rice

PREPARATION

1. Clean and shell prawns; leave the tail shells on. Slit them down the back to remove the vein and then flatten them into butterfly shapes. Coat the prawns and fish fillets in flour.

2. Peel carrot and cut it into thick julienne strips about 2 inchs long.

3. Combine flour and egg mixture and stir very lightly. Do not beat: the lumps will take care of themselves. (Note: ½ tsp vinegar added to

the batter makes it light and flaky.)

4. In a deep skillet heat cooking oil to 350 degrees. The heat is right when batter dropped into it floats quickly to the surface and remains there spinning about. Holding the prawns by the tails, dip them one by one in batter and then lower them into hot oil. Fry till golden and done; remove and drain. Repeat with the fish fillets and then with the carrot sticks. Drain on paper towels; do not allow the pieces to overlap, for this makes them soggy.

5. Place a generous serving of rice in each of four rice bowls. Top with prawns, fish, and carrot. Make a sauce by combining stock, soy sauce, monosodium glutamate, and mirin and bringing the mixture quickly to boil. Pour about 1 tbsp of the sauce over each serving of fried seafood and rice. Serve immediately.

Korea

The cuisines of China and Japan have influenced them, but Korean foods are truly distinctive. Though less splended in variety than the extensive range of Chinese food, Korean dishes are nonetheless hearty and nutritious. Koreanbarbecued meats—especially beef—make an excellent dish for convivial gatherings because they are eaten from the grill as they are cooked. In addition to thinly sliced pork and beef, Korean restaurants often include in their barbecues, liver, stomach, and other internal organs. The delicious spicy pickles given in this section are an essential accompaniment to Korean barbecued foods.

The three basic spices used in almost all Korean dishes are sesame seeds, red chili peppers, and garlic, the so-called three flavors. In addition to these, however, ginger, sesame oil, and leeks are popular. Perhaps the most famous of all Korean foods are the pickles called kimchi. Made from such raw vegetables as Chinese cabbage, cucumbers, and turnips, these pickles are highly and hotly seasoned with garlic and pepper. Though many people find them too fiery for consumption alone, servings of boiled or steamed rice modulate the spiciness and enable one to savor the taste and aroma of the pickles. The sesame-seed cookies and ginger tea on p. 136 are a delicious finale to almost any meal.

In general, Korean food is easy to prepare, requires no difficult-to-obtain ingredients, and appeals to almost everyone. You will find that it is an excellent addition to your culinary repertory.

Rice and Barley

(4 servings)

INGREDIENTS
1½ cups rice   4 cups water
½ cup pearl barley

1. Add 2 cups boiling water to the barley and soak for 12 hours. Bring to a boil, lower heat, and simmer for 30 minutes.

2. Wash rice well until water runs clear. Drain, let stand for from 30 minutes to 1 hour. Combine rice and barley.

3. Add 2 cups water, cover tightly, and bring to a boil. Reduce the heat to as low as possible and continue to cook for 20 minutes. Do not stir or open lid during cooking. Remove from heat and let stand covered for about 15 minutes.

Rice and Dates

(4 servings)

INGREDIENTS

2 cups rice   2¾ cups cold water
½ cup seeded dates

PREPARATION

1. Wash rice well until water runs clear. Drain; let stand for from 30 minutes to 1 hour.

2. Quarter the dates.

3. Add dates and 2¾ cups cold water to the rice. Let stand 30 minutes.

4. Cover tightly and bring to a boil. Reduce heat to as low as possible and continue to cook for 10 minutes. Do not stir or remove the lid during cooking. Turn flame off and let stand covered for about 15 minutes.

Rice and Vegetables

(10-12 servings)

INGREDIENTS

4 cups rice   3 tsp vegetable oil
4 cups cold water   6 tbsp soy sauce
½ lb beef   2 cups celery cut in 1-inch lengths
3 green onions   1 carrot
1½ cloves garlic   2 cucumbers
3 tbsp parched white sesame seeds   10 oz bean sprouts

2 eggs	½ tsp salt
10 oz snow peas	½ tsp pepper
½ tsp monosodium glutamate	

PREPARATION

1. Wash the rice in cold water and rub between the fingers to remove all surface starch. Continue washing until the water runs clear. Drain thoroughly.

2. Add cold water. Cover tightly and bring quickly to a boil. Reduce heat to as low as possible and steam 30 minutes. Do not stir or remove the lid during cooking.

3. Grind or chop the beef fine. Mince 2 green onions and 1 clove garlic. Add this to the beef. Add pepper, 2 tbsp sesame seeds, 1 tsp oil, and 4 tbsp soy sauce. Mix well. Stirring constantly, cook slowly until meat is done.

4. Wash the cucumber. Without peeling it, cut into 1-inch lengths and shred each piece lengthwise. Sprinkle with salt and let stand 10 minutes. Press out any water that forms. Heat ½ tsp oil in a frying pan. Sauté cucumber for 2 minutes.

5. Shred each piece of celery lengthwise. Sprinkle with salt and let stand 10 minutes. Press out any water that forms and sauté in ½ tsp oil for 2 minutes.

6. Wash then peel the carrot. Cut into 1-inch lengths and shred each piece lengthwise. Cook for 3 minutes in boiling salted water. Drain.

7. If you are using fresh bean sprouts wash them in cold water and parboil until just tender. Drain. Add 2 tbsp soy sauce, 1 chopped green onion, ½ chopped garlic clove, 1 tsp oil, and 1 tbsp parched sesame seeds. Mix well and cook until all ingredients are well seasoned.

8. Separate 2 eggs. Beat both yolks and eggs lightly with chopsticks or a fork. Cook the white by pouring a small amount into a thin layer in the bottom of an oiled, heated skillet. When firm, turn and cook lightly on the other side. Cook the yolk in the same way. Roll each layer separately into a long cylinder and shred as thin as possible.

9. Cook snow peas in boiling salted water ½ minute. Rinse in cold water and drain well; shred. Reserve peas, egg, cucumber, and ½ of the carrot. Add other prepared foods to the rice, mixing lightly. Serve in bowls or on plates. Decorate with peas, egg, cucumber, and carrot.

Broiled Pork

(4 servings)

INGREDIENTS

1 lb pork sliced thin
½ cup soy sauce
2 tbsp sugar
1 green onion minced
1 clove garlic minced
4 tbsp parched and crushed
    sesame seeds

1 tsp sesame oil
½ tsp salt
½ tsp black pepper
½ tsp monosodium glutamate
1 tsp chopped candied ginger

PREPARATION

1. Place the pork in a deep bowl and sprinkle it with soy sauce, sugar, minced onion, minced garlic, chopped ginger, sesame seeds, salt, and freshly ground black pepper. Toss with a spoon to coat the pork evenly. Set aside to marinate at room temperature for about 30 minutes or in the refrigerator for about 1 hour. Turn the pieces of meat occasionally to keep them moist.

2. Broil the pork or fry it in a small amount of oil. If you fry it, cover tightly after the meat is well browned. Add a small amount of water and steam until the pork is tender. Add monosodium glutamate and serve with hot rice.

Broiled Beef

(4 servings)

INGREDIENTS

2 lb beef
1 clove garlic minced
2 tbsp parched white sesame
    seeds
2½ tbsp sugar
½ tbsp honey
½ cup soy sauce

4 tbsp green onion minced
1 tsp red chili pepper minced
1 tbsp fresh ginger juice
1 tbsp sesame oil
½ tsp salt
½ tsp monosodium glutamate
1 tbsp cornstarch

PREPARATION

1. Cut the beef into thin slices 3 inches square.

2. Combine sugar, honey, soy sauce, onion, garlic, sesame seeds, salt, monosodium glutamate, chili pepper, ginger juice and oil. Combine this mixture and 1 tbsp cornstarch with the meat. Mix well and let stand for 15 minutes.

3. Broil on a charcoal fire or in a well heated broiler. Serve hot with rice.

Hot Pot

This elaborate and delicious one-dish meal is reserved for special occasions. Its name derives from that of the pot in which it is cooked. The same kind of pot, which is called by a variety of names in Japan and China, is metal. It has a cover and a kind of chimney in the center into which one puts glowing charcoal to complete the cooking and heating of the already partly prepared ingredients. Modern electric versions are available. (see p. 34)

(4–6 servings)

INGREDIENTS

½ lb beef, sirloin or tenderloin	4 tbsp cornstarch
3 tsp sugar	3 eggs
½ cup soy sauce	1 bunch spinach
2 cloves garlic mashed	3 fresh mushrooms
pepper	2 tbsp pine nuts
2 tbsp parched sesame seeds	9 pistachio nuts
4 tbsp vegetable oil	2 walnuts
about ⅛ lb liver	3 medium turnips peeled
salt	

PREPARATION

1. Cut ¼ of the beef into thin slices 3 by 5 inches. Combine 1 tsp sugar, 1 tbsp soy sauce, ½ clove mashed garlic, pepper, sesame seeds, and 1 tsp oil. Marinate meat in this mixture for 30 minutes.

2. Fry marinated meat in a small amout of oil until tender. Cut it into pieces 1 inch wide and as long as the radius of the pot in which it will be cooked.

3. Chop another ¼ of the beef very fine. Add 2 tbsp soy sauce, 1 tbsp parched sesame seeds, ½ clove mashed garlic, 1 tsp oil, and pepper. Mix well. Roll the mixture into tiny balls. Enclose 1 pine nut in the center

of each ball. Roll in cornstarch and dip in lightly beaten egg. Lightly brown the meatballs in a small amount of vegetable oil.

4. Cut $\frac{1}{2}$ of the beef into thin strips 2 inch long and $\frac{1}{2}$ inch wide. Combine with 3 tbsp soy sauce, 2 tsp sugar, 1 tsp parched sesame seeds, pepper, 1 clove mashed garlic, and $\frac{1}{2}$ tbsp oil. Mix well.

5. Drop the liver into boiling water and cook 3 minutes. Remove, skin, and cut into thin strips $\frac{1}{2}$ inch wide. Sprinkle with salt, dip in cornstarch then in lightly beaten egg. Sauté in a small amount of oil until tender.

6. Remove stems from spinach; blanch leaves in boiling water until just limp. Carefully stack leaves $\frac{1}{2}$ inch deep. Dip in cornstarch to coat then in the beaten egg. Sauté the spinach stacks in oil until lightly browned, then cut each into slices about $1\frac{1}{2}$ inches wide.

7. Slice mushrooms and sauté lightly in oil.

8. Separate the yolk and white of 1 egg. Add a pinch of salt and $\frac{1}{4}$ tsp cornstarch to each and beat lightly with a chopstick or fork. Cook separately by pouring small amounts of each in the bottom of a heated, oiled skillet. When firm, turn and cook slightly on other side. Cut the egg in pieces $\frac{1}{2}$ inch wide and as long as the pieces of liver.

9. Prepare 1 hard-boiled egg. Remove the shell and cut off the ends of the egg. Cut the center into three slices to be used for decoration.

10. Shell and blanch the pistachio nuts. Shell and remove the skins from the remaining pine nuts. Carefully shell the walnuts so that the halves are not broken; blanch.

11. Wash, peel, and boil the turnips whole in $1\frac{1}{2}$ cups of salted water. When turnips are tender, pour off and reserve the liquid. Cut the turnips in pieces $1\frac{1}{2}$ inch long, 1 inch wide, $\frac{1}{4}$ inch thick.

12. After all the food is prepared, arrange it in the pot as follows. In the bottom, place a layer of fried egg, mushrooms, liver, and beef. Continue with these layers until the pot is filled. Then place the tiny meat balls around the center stem of the pot. Decorate with 3 slices of hard-boiled egg, walnuts, pine nuts, and pistachio nuts. Add the water in which the turnips were cooked. Place the lid on the pot and fill the center with glowing charcoal.

Set the cooking pot in the middle of the table. Bring the liquid in the pot to a boil and simmer for several minutes. Remove the cover. Allow guests to help themselves from the pot, using chopsticks or forks. After all foods have been eaten, ladle broth into soup bowls for sipping.

Beef Pok-kum

(4 servings)

INGREDIENTS

¼ lb ground beef
½ large mushroom
2 tbsp soy sauce
1 chopped green onion
1 clove garlic minced
pepper
1 egg

1 tbsp sesame seed coarsely
  ground
1 tsp sesame oil
½ minced ginger root
½ tsp salt
¼ cup water

PREPARATION

1. Slice the mushroom. Combine the soy sauce, chopped onion, chopped ginger, garlic, pepper, ground sesame seed, and oil. Add this and the mushrooms to the meat. Mix well and sauté in a small amount of oil for 5 minutes.

2. Season with salt. Add water and continue cooking until ingredients are done.

3. Add a lightly beaten egg to the mixture just before serving.

Broiled Chicken

(4 servings)

INGREDIENTS

1 fryer chicken
4 tbsp soy sauce
2 tbsp parched sesame seeds
pepper
1 chopped green onion

1 clove garlic mashed
1 tbsp sugar
1 tsp sesame oil
2 tbsp vegetable oil

PREPARATION

1. Clean, skin, and bone the chicken. Flatten the meat and cut it into squares ⅛ inch thick and about 2 or 3 inches to a side.

2. Combine soy sauce, sesame seeds, pepper, chopped onion, garlic, sugar, and oil.

3. Add the chicken, mix well, and marinate for 30 minutes.

4. Remove the chicken from marinade. Drain well. Broil on a barbecue grill or fry slowly in a frying pan with 2 tbsp salad oil. After it is

well browned, add a small amount of water, cover tightly, and steam until tender.

Chicken Pok-kum

(4 servings)

INGREDIENTS

1 chicken	3 tbsp sesame seeds crushed
½ cup soy sauce	2 tbsp sugar
2 green onions chopped	4 dried shiitake mushrooms
2 cloves garlic mashed	salt
pepper	½ tsp monosodium glutamate

PREPARATION

1. Clean the chicken, wipe it dry, and, using a heavy knife, cut it into 1½-inch squares.
2. Cover with boiling water and simmer slowly until partly done.
3. Soften dried mushrooms in ¼ cup water. Remove and discard stem. Slice.
4. Combine soy sauce, chopped onion, garlic, pepper, sesame seeds, and sugar. Mix well.
5. Remove chicken from broth and add it to the combined seasonings. Add sliced mushrooms and enough of the broth to half cover the chicken. Continue simmering until the chicken is very tender.

Short-rib Barbecue

(4–6 servings)

INGREDIENTS

2 lbs short ribs	½ tsp pepper
3 tbsp sugar	2 tbsp parched sesame seeds crushed
2 tbsp vegetable oil	
4 tbsp light soy sauce	1 tbsp sake
2 tbsp dark soy sauce	1 tbsp mirin (see p. 201)
1 green onion chopped	1 tsp red chili pepper chopped
1 clove garlic mashed	

1. Have the butcher cut ribs into serving pieces (about 3 inch cubes). With bone side down, score in the following way. Cut cubes halfway to bone every $\frac{1}{2}$ inch in one direction; at right angles to the first incisions, cut every $\frac{1}{2}$ inch to a depth of only $\frac{1}{2}$ inch.

2. Add sugar and oil to the ribs. Mix well and let stand while preparing the remaining marinade ingredients. Combine soy sauces, chopped onion, garlic, peppers, sesame seed, sake, and mirin.

3. Put scored rib sections into marinade. Cover and refrigerate for from 1 to 3 hours.

4. Place meat, bone side down, on barbecue grill over medium heat. Brown each side for about 10 to 15 minutes. Brush with marinade as meat cooks. The charcoal fire may be prepared and placed conveniently near the serving table. A Genghis Khan grill, ordinary Japanese hibachi, or other barbecue may be used.

Boiled Fish with Vegetables

(6 servings)

INGREDIENTS

1 (2 lb) white-flesh fish
$\frac{1}{4}$ lb beef
6 green onions cut in 2-inch lengths
1 clove garlic chopped
1 tbsp sesame seed
$\frac{1}{2}$ cup mushrooms sliced
$\frac{1}{2}$ cup bamboo shoots sliced thin

1 carrot cut into julienne strips $1\frac{1}{2}$ inches long
4 stalks celery in 2-inch julienne strips
3 tbsp oil
1 green onion minced
4 tbsp soy sauce
1 tbsp sugar
1 tsp chopped chili pepper
2 pieces candied ginger chopped

PREPARATION

1. Clean, bone, and cut fish into 2- or 3-inch squares.

2. Slice beef thin. Add sugar, 2 tbsp soy sauce, green onion, garlic, sesame seeds, pepper, and oil. Mix well.

3. Heat oil in a frying pan. Arrange sliced beef in a single layer. Then add layers of bamboo shoot, celery, mushrooms, carrots, and fish.

4. Sprinkle a layer of onion, chopped chili pepper, and small pieces of chopped ginger over the fish.

5. Repeat until all ingredients are used then add water (to cover half the fish and vegetable mixture), and remaining 2 tbsp soy sauce. Cover and simmer over medium heat 8-10 minutes or until done.

6. Arrange in a large bowl, sprinkle with minced green onion, and serve.

Mushroom Soup

(6 servings)

INGREDIENTS

$\frac{1}{4}$ lb beef
2 green onions
1 cup sliced mushrooms
1 large carrot
1 clove garlic chopped

1 tbsp parched sesame seeds
7 cups chicken broth
4 tbsp soy sauce
dash salt and pepper
$\frac{1}{4}$ tsp monosodium glutamate

PREPARATION

1. Cut beef into thin slices 1 inch square. Add 2 tbsp soy sauce, onions, garlic, sesame seeds, pepper, and mushrooms. Mix well.

2. Wash and scrape the carrot. Cut into $\frac{1}{8}$-inch slices. Add them to the meat mixture.

3. In a heavy saucepan heat a small amount of oil and sauté the meat mixture in it. Add chicken broth, remaining 2 tbsp soy sauce, and monosodium glutamate. Season with salt and serve.

Turnip Pickles

INGREDIENTS

12 medium turnips
2 red chili peppers
3 tbsp salt

2 tsp candied ginger
3 cups cold water

PREPARATION

1. Wash, peel, and quarter turnips. Sprinkle 2 tbsp salt on them and let stand 2 days. Reserve salt water from turnips.

2. Slice turnips in $\frac{1}{2}$-inch slices.

134

3. Put turnips in a jar or bowl with a tightly fitting cover. Add chopped ginger, chopped red pepper, 1 tbsp salt, salt water from turnips, plus enough extra water to make 3 cups. Mix well and refrigerate for 2 weeks. Serve the marinade with the turnips.

Chinese-cabbage Pickles

INGREDIENTS

1 head Chinese cabbage
6 tbsp salt
6 green onions
2 cloves garlic minced

1 tsp chopped red chili peppers
2 tsp chopped candied ginger
3 cups cold water

PREPARATION

1. Wash the cabbage in cold running water and dry with paper towels. Cut it into pieces 1 inch by 1 inch. Sprinkle with 4 tbsp salt. Mix well and let stand 15 minutes.
2. Cut the green onion into 1½-inch lengths and shred lengthwise.
3. Wash cabbage in cold running water and dry with paper towels.
4. Mix the prepared onion, garlic, red chili pepper, and ginger with the cabbage. Add 2 tbsp salt and put into a glass jar or bowl. Add enough water to cover the cabbage. Cover tightly and marinate for several days in the refrigerator.

Cucumber Pickles

INGREDIENTS

6 large cucumbers
3 tbsp salt
2 green onions

1 clove garlic minced
1 tsp chopped red chili pepper
1 cup cold water

PREPARATION

1. Wash the cucumbers and cut into 1½-inch lengths. Cut each of the pieces in half lengthwise and remove the seeds. Add 2 tbsp salt to the cucumbers. Mix well and let stand 15 minutes.
2. Cut the onion into 1½-inch lengths and shred each piece lengthwise.
3. Wash cucumbers. Combine them with onion, garlic, red chili

pepper, 1 tbsp salt, and water. Mix well. Marinate in refrigerator for from 2 days to 1 week.

Sesame-seed Cookies

(4 dozen)

INGREDIENTS

2¼ cups sifted, all-purpose flour
1 tsp baking powder
¼ tsp salt
1 stick of butter (½ cup)
¼ tsp salt
¾ cup sugar

1 egg
½ cup parched sesame seeds
2 tbsp cold water
additional sesame seeds for
   topping

PREPARATION

1. Sift together flour, baking powder, and salt. Cream the butter and add to it sugar, egg, and sesame seeds. Mix well.

2. Add flour mixture alternately with water. Mix well.

3. Shape into an oblong about 2 inches wide and 2 inches thick. Wrap in foil and chill until firm.

4. Cut into ⅛ inch slices and put on greased cookie sheets. Sprinkle with more seeds. Press seeds into the dough. Bake in a preheated moderate (350°) oven for 12 to 15 minutes.

Ginger Tea

(5 servings)

INGREDIENTS

⅓ cup sliced, fresh ginger
5 cups water
2 dates (oriental dates)
3 walnuts

1 tbsp pine nuts
¾ cup sugar
½ tsp cinnamon

PREPARATION

1. Wash and scrape the skin from the ginger. Slice it very thin. Add 5 cups of water and boil for 20 minutes.

2. Thinly slice the dates. Shell and blanch the walnut meats; cut

them into small pieces. Shell the pine nuts.

3. Add sugar and cinnamon to the water in which the ginger was cooked.

4. Place a small amount of dates, walnuts, and pine nuts in each cup. Pour in ginger tea and serve hot.

Philippine Islands

The Philippine cuisine is highly diverse and includes fine foods from many countries. I have selected only the ones that I consider most representative of the Philippine approach to eating. In addition to the famous lumpia, which I have included, the Philippines are noted for lechon, whole barbecued pig. Since this is generally impractical to prepare in the private home, I have omitted it; but I strongly recommend that if you have an opportunity to sample it you do so; it is a great treat. Because of the historical experience of the islands, Spanish influence is apparent in much Philippine food. Escabesche, a marinated fish delicacy popular in many Mediterranean countries, is a favorite in the Philippines as well. In spite of a pronounced Latin quality, however, many Philippine foods are distinctive and excellent in their own right. From the several dishes deserving special attention I offer a few that are easy to prepare, appealing, and nutritious.

As is true throughout most of the Orient, rice is a staple in the Philippines. It is eaten alone or with other foods at almost all meals. Seafoods rank second in the Philippine diet, which also includes pork, chicken, vegetables, and fruits. Adobo, highly spiced meats, poultry, or seafood, and lumpia, a Philippine version of Chinese egg rolls, are great favorites. These and other dishes are often accompanied by delicious Philippine beer or an alcoholic beverage called luba and made from fermented coconut juice.

Egg Rolls (Lumpia)

(6 servings)

INGREDIENTS
LUMPIA FILLING (4½ cups)
1 lb ground pork   ½ lb shelled shrimp chopped

1½ cups coconut (southern style if available)
4 large cloves garlic minced
1 onion chopped

2 tbsp cooking oil
1½ tsp salt
1 tsp monosodium glutamate
1 tsp sugar

LUMPIA WRAPPINGS (18)
1½ cups water
¾ cup cornstarch
3 eggs well beaten

¾ tsp salt
5 tsp vegetable oil

PREPARATION

1. Heat oil in large skillet over moderate heat. Sauté garlic and onions until tender. Add and sauté pork until completely cooked, stirring occasionally. Add shrimp and continue cooking until shrimp turn pink. Add coconut; cook over low heat 2 more minutes.

2. Add remaining ingredients, stir well, and remove from heat. Set aside to cool.

3. Prepare lumpia wrappings in this way. In a bowl gradually add water to cornstarch to make a smooth paste. Add remaining ingredients. Mix well. Oil a 6-inch skillet. Pour about 3 tbsp batter into pan, tipping to make a thin crêpe. Cook on one side; remove. When all are cooked and filling is cool, place about ¼ cup of filling on each wrapping. Fold to enclose filling and serve with lumpia sauce (see below).

LUMPIA SAUCE
(3 cups)
2 cloves garlic mashed
1 tbsp vegetable oil
4 tbsp cornstarch

⅓ cup brown sugar
½ cup soy sauce
2½ cups water

1. Heat oil and sauté garlic until brown. Remove from pan. Reserve.

2. Combine cornstarch with water; blend thoroughly. Add sugar and remaining ingredients. Pour into pan. Simmer, stirring constantly, until sauce thickens. Remove from heat and serve topped with garlic.

Spiced Pork Marinated in Soy Sauce and Garlic

(16 servings)

INGREDIENTS
8 lbs fresh ham

6 cloves garlic finely minced

2 cups cider vinegar
1 cup soy sauce
2 tsp salt
1½ tsp pepper

2 cups beer (preferably Philippine beer)
4 cups water
3 cups boiling water

PREPARATION

1. Combine garlic, vinegar, soy sauce, salt, and pepper. Marinate fresh ham in this mixture for 1 hour.

2. Place pork in a large pot, add 4 cups water and 2 cups of beer. Cover tightly and simmer until tender (about 4 hours).

3. Degrease. Add 3 cups boiling water and simmer 20 minutes. The pork must be brown on all sides. This is a delicious at-home party dish served hot or cold.

Spiced Chicken Marinated in Soy Sauce and Garlic

(4-6 servings)

INGREDIENTS

1 chicken
1 clove garlic minced
½ tsp whole peppercorns
½ cup cider vinegar

1 cup beer (preferably Philippine beer)
½ bay leaf
vegetable oil
salt and pepper to taste

PREPARATION

1. Clean the chicken and cut into serving pieces. Add salt and pepper to taste, garlic, peppercorns, bay leaf, vinegar, and beer. Cover and simmer until the meat is tender and the liquid has evaporated (about 30 minutes).

2. Heat a little vegetable oil in a 10-inch skillet over moderate heat until a light haze forms above it. Add chicken and fry until browned. Serve hot or cold.

Sweet Rice Flour and Coconut Dessert

INGREDIENTS

1 lb sweet rice flour

½ can frozen coconut milk

140

3 tbsp shredded coconut
oil

1 lb brown sugar
3 tbsp water

PREPARATION

1. Combine sweet rice flour, coconut milk, and shredded coconut. Shape into balls about 1 inch in diameter.

2. Heat oil to about 350° and fry sweet rice balls for about 5 minutes or until puffed and brown.

3. Make a heavy sirup by placing about 3 tbsp water in a heavy skillet and stirring in 1 lb brown sugar. Stirring constantly cook over a low heat until the sugar is caramelized. Place the hot coconut balls in the sirup and stir then gently until lightly coated.

Beef and Vegetables

(6-8 servings)

INGREDIENTS

2 lbs stew beef
2 cups beer
1 clove garlic minced
¼ cup vegetable oil
1 large onion chopped
½ cup tomato purée
½ head cabbage quartered

2 potatoes quartered
½ lb green beans cut in 1-inch
  pieces
2 bananas
½ cup halved Vienna sausages
salt and pepper
1 cup garbanzo beans

PREPARATION

1. Combine beef and beer in a pot, adding only enough water to cover meat. Bring to a boil and simmer until tender (about 1 hour).

2. Heat oil and sauté garlic and onion until brown. Add tomato purée, potatoes, cabbage, and green beans. Pour in 1 cup of water; simmer until potatoes are tender and the sauce is thick. Add water during cooking if necessary. Add garbanzo beans (cooked or canned) and sausages and continue cooking until all ingredients are heated.

3. Cut bananas in diagonal slices and drop into boiling water just long enough to heat.

4. After seasoning cooked beef with salt and pepper, add vegetables. Gently mix in the bananas.

Indonesia and Southeast Asia

Indonesian food is probably best known for the famous rice table or rijstafel, which is no more than a number of the dishes presented here served with plates of steamed rice. Each guest selects portions of curries, vegetables, and other condiments and places them on the rice, which he eats as an accompaniment to the foods. Rice tables frequently include chicken sate, curries, and the kind of condiments often found with Indian curries: diced tomatoes, sautéed onion rings, chopped peanuts, coconut, diced green peppers, and so on. The variety of things to be served with the rice is limited only by the imagination of the cook.

Southeast Asian food is represented here by only a few dishes, which, though limited in number, are delicious and easy to prepare. The curried foods popular in Thailand, Cambodia, and Vietnam are often fiery in the extreme. I have not included these dishes since Indonesian and Indian curries, though perhaps slightly different because of variations in local ingredients, are sufficient to give the Western cook an idea of the wide possibilities of curry cooking.

In the diet of Southeast Asia fruit plays an important part. Bananas of many kinds, coconut, mangoes, mangosteens, durian, and pineapple of delicate sweetness and unexcelled flavor are used throughout the area. There is no need to give recipes for these fruits, since they are usually eaten raw as is fitting to their excellence.

Indonesia

Yellow Rice

(4 servings)

INGREDIENTS

2 cups rice
3 cups milk
1 tsp turmeric powder
1 bay leaf
½ tsp salt

3 or 4 celery leaves
2 red chili peppers
½ small cucumber
1 onion cut in thin rings
2 eggs

PREPARATION

1. Combine turmeric, bay leaf, salt, and milk and bring to a boil. Remove the bay leaf.

2. Wash the rice and stir milk into it. Allow this mixture to stand for 30 minutes.

3. Cook till milk is absorbed then steam till the rice is ready to serve.

4. Cut the chili peppers into flower shapes and the cucumber into slices. Sauté the onion rings. Prepare a thin omelet with the eggs and cut it into fine strips.

5. Garnish the cooked rice with peppers, cucumber, onion rings, celery leaves, and omelet strips.

Chicken Sate

(4-6 servings)

INGREDIENTS

1 chicken (3 to 3½ lb)
1 tsp black pepper
1 red chili chopped

3 cloves garlic minced
4 tbsp peanut butter
1 chicken bouillon cube

juice of 1 lemon
¼ tsp salt

1 cup ketchup
metal skewers

PREPARATION

1. Cut the chicken into small pieces. Remove the bones and skin. Combine black pepper, salt, and ketchup; mix to a fine paste. Coat the chicken thoroughly with this paste. Store in refrigerator for 24 hours. When you are ready to cook the sate, skewer 5 small pieces of chicken on each of as many skewers as are needed.

2. To make sate sauce pound together red chili, garlic, and peanut butter. Mix into a sauce with lemon juice and bouillon cube dissolved in a little water. If the sauce is too thick, dilute with more chicken stock. This may be stored in refrigerator or frozen until you are ready to use it.

3. Brush meat with oil and broil over charcoal. Turn and baste with paste several times during cooking. Broil about 10 minutes or till chicken is done. Serve with sate sauce. Add more lemon juice if needed.

Chicken or Mutton Sate

(4-6 servings)

INGREDIENTS

2 lbs boned and skinned chicken
   or mutton
2 walnuts crushed
1 green onion minced
1 inch fresh ginger root scraped
   and grated

1 large clove garlic minced
juice of 1 lemon or 1 tsp
   tamarind juice
salt

SATE SAUCE

2 tbsp butter
½ cup roasted peanuts
1 green chili chopped
1½ tsp soy sauce
1 small onion grated

1 medium onion sliced fine
1 tbsp coconut cooking oil
juice of 1 lime or lemon
salt and monosodium glutamate
   to taste

PREPARATION

1. Cut the chicken or mutton into 1-inch cubes. Combine walnuts,

144

green onions, ginger, garlic, and lemon juice with a pinch of salt. Grind or crush the mixture and rub it thoroughly into the chicken or mutton. Allow it to stand for 1 hour.

2. Melt butter in a frying pan. Sauté sliced onion till brown. Remove and reserve.

3. Remove the thin skins from the peanuts and grind them. Grind the chili and the small onion together. Sauté in hot coconut oil. After 3 minutes, add peanuts and salt. Since the fried mixture will be thick, add a little warm water to make a smooth sauce.

4. Remove from the heat; mix in soy sauce and lemon juice. Pour over the chicken or mutton. Sprinkle fried onions over the dish and serve.

Rice and Meat in Banana Leaves

INGREDIENTS

3 cups glutinous rice
1 cup coconut milk
$\frac{1}{4}$ tsp saffron
1 lb ground chicken
3 minced green onions
2 red chili peppers finely
   chopped

1 tomato peeled, seeded, and
   diced
1 tsp salt
20 6-inch squares cut from
   banana leaves
2$\frac{1}{2}$ tbsp coconut oil
dash monosodium glutamate
20 toothpicks

PREPARATION

1. Wash rice with cold water and rub the grains lightly between your fingers to remove all surface starch. Change the water 4 or 5 time until it runs clear. Drain rice thoroughly. Place saffron in a bowl, pour in 2 cups water and 1 cup coconut milk. Soak rice in this mixture overnight and then drain.

2. Steam rice in an oriental steamer or place it in a metal colander set in a large pot containing 1$\frac{1}{2}$ inches of water. Bring the water to a boil over high heat. Place a piece of gauze over the colander and spread the rice on it. Cover the pan tightly and steam for about 45 minutes.

3. Heat coconut oil in a skillet. Sauté green onions, chili peppers, ground chicken, and tomato. Continue cooking; add 1 tsp salt and a dash of monosodium glutamate.

4. On each banana-leaf square place a portion of rice and chicken mixture. Fold square from left to right and fasten ends with toothpicks.

5. Steam over high heat and serve hot.

Trout Curry

(4 servings)

INGREDIENTS

2 fresh cleaned trout

2 tbsp olive oil

$\frac{1}{2}$ cup milk

4 tomatoes

1 small head lettuce

1 to 2 red chili peppers

1 large onion chopped

$\frac{1}{4}$ tsp coriander seeds ground

1 egg beaten

4 cloves garlic chopped

salt and pepper to taste

parsley

cabbage leaves

PREPARATION

1. Wash the fish and tap gently with the back of a heavy wooden spoon or a meat mallet to loosen the skin. Carefully remove the flesh with as little damage to the skin as possible.

2. Bone the flesh thoroughly and chop it fine.

3. Mix the fish with the coriander, onion, garlic, egg, milk, pepper, and salt.

4. Fill the fish skins with this stuffing. Wrap each fish in cabbage leaves and steam for 20 minutes.

5. In a heavy 10-inch skillet heat olive oil over moderate heat until it is very hot but not smoking. Fry the fish till brown and serve garnished with small pieces of red pepper, tomato, lettuce, and parsley.

Simple Fish Curry

(4 servings)

INGREDIENTS

4 cod (or other fish) fillets
2 tsp butter or vegetable oil
1 cup coconut milk
1 tbsp garam massala (see p. 210)

6 onions sliced fine
2 tbsp thick tamarind juice,
   or puréed apricots
salt

PREPARATION

1. Sprinkle the fish lightly on both sides with salt, fry in half the butter and set aside.

2. Put the coconut milk in a heavy saucepan. Add to it 2 tsp butter or oil, garam massala, and sliced onions. Mix well then add the fish and bring to a boil. Simmer gently for 15 minutes. Add the tamarind juice, simmer for two more minutes. Serve at once.

Fish Curry

(4 servings)

INGREDIENTS

1 lb white-flesh fish cut into
   pieces
1 cup coconut milk
½ tsp ground cumin
6 peppercorns
1 ½ ground turmeric
½ tsp ground ginger
6 cloves of garlic mashed

2 red chilis or ½ tsp ground
   chili powder
½ tsp fenugreek
2 tbsp butter or vegetable oil
½–1 tsp salt
juice or pulp of 6 tamarind
   pods (lemon juice or puréed
   apricots)

PREPARATION

1. In a heavy 10-inch skillet heat butter or vegetable oil over moderate heat until a light haze forms above it. Add the fenugreek and sauté for 2 minutes.

2. Add garlic, salt, and spices; brown. Put in the fish plus ½ cup water.

3. Simmer for 10 minutes, add tamarind juice or pulp. Just before serving, add coconut milk and mix well.

Prawn Curry 1

(4 servings)

INGREDIENTS

1 lb prawns
1 cup of coconut milk
2 red chilis ground
1 inch fresh ginger grated
6 cloves garlic mashed
2 tbsp ground coriander
1 inch turmeric or 1 tsp turmeric
  powder

$\frac{1}{2}$ tsp ground cumin seed
2 tbsp vegetable oil
1 onion sliced
1 tbsp tamarind juice (lemon
  juice)
$\frac{1}{2}$–1 tsp salt

PREPARATION

1. Carefully shell the prawns, but leave the last shell segment and the tail attached. Devein the prawns. Wash prawns with cold water and pat dry with paper towels.

2. Heat vegetable oil in a 10-inch skillet. Add onions and stir till they are golden. Put the prawns into the skillet, stir-fry for 3 minutes. When the prawns turn pink, sprinkle them with salt and a mixture of chilis, ginger, garlic, coriander, turmeric, and cumin.

3. Dilute half the coconut milk with an equal amount of water and pour over the prawns.

4. Simmer till tender. Add tamarind or lemon juice and the remainder of the coconut milk. Serve hot.

Prawn Curry 2

(4 servings)

INGREDIENTS

1 lb prawns shelled and deveined
$\frac{1}{2}$ cup dried coconut
$\frac{1}{2}$ tsp turmeric
1 tsp chili powder
2 tbsp yogurt
1 large onion chopped

5 cloves of garlic mashed
$\frac{1}{2}$ tbsp peanut oil
salt to taste
$\frac{1}{2}$ lemon
$\frac{1}{2}$ tsp fenugreek

PREPARATION

1. Sauté the chopped onions in oil. When they are golden add 1 cup water and all remaining ingredients except prawns and lemon.

2. Simmer for 10 minutes.

3. Add prawns and the juice of $\frac{1}{2}$ lemon.

4. Simmer for another 10 minutes and serve.

Southeast Asia

Beef with Coconut Cream

(6 servings)

INGREDIENTS

2 lbs beef cut in thin strips
2 cups coconut milk
1 tsp brown sugar
1 tbsp anchovy paste
1 tsp crushed chili pepper
1 onion minced
½ cup ground peanuts
6 cloves garlic minced
1 tsp ground turmeric

1 blade lemon grass or 1 tsp
 grated lemon rind
2 tbsp cooking oil
¼ cup all-purpose flour
2 tbsp water
1 bunch watercress
¼ cup coconut cream
 (see coconut; p. 197)

PREPARATION

1. Simmer beef in coconut milk to which have been added brown sugar and anchory paste. Sauté chili pepper, onion, peanuts, garlic, turmeric, and lemon grass or lemon rind in oil. Add to the meat mixture.

2. Thicken with flour mixed with 2 tbsp water. Cover and bring to a boil. Simmer for 5 minutes.

3. Cut watercress into 2-inch lengths. Wash; without draining put in a pot. Cover and wilt over low heat. Plunge immediately in cold water. Drain and arrange in a ring on a platter, place the meat and sauce in the center and cover with coconut cream beaten till frothy.

Chicken Curry with Pulwal

(4 servings)

INGREDIENTS

1 dozen pulwal (large pea pods or okra)
1 chicken

4 tbsp coconut oil or other
  cooking oil
½ medium sized onion grated
1 tsp ground turmeric
1 tsp ground chili powder
½ tsp fresh ground ginger

2 blades lemon grass or 1
  tbsp grated lemon rind
½ tsp garlic powder
2 cups coconut milk
3 or 4 cloves
3 or 4 ground cardamons
1-inch stick of cinnamon ground

PREPARATION

1. Bone and mince the meat from a plump chicken.

2. Heat oil in a small pan and briefly sauté onions, turmeric, chili, ginger, garlic, cloves, cardamon, and cinnamon.

3. Combine chicken with this mixture.

4. Wash pulwal; slit them down one side and scrape out seeds. Stuff pulwal with the chicken meat, join the sides and tie with cotton string.

5. Simmer for 30–40 minutes in coconut milk to which has been added 2 blades of lemon grass. Remove lemon grass. Serve with rice.

Fried Duck in Ginger Sauce

(4 servings)

INGREDIENTS

1 duck (3 or 4 lbs)
¾ cup water
½ cup sugar
½ cup vinegar
1 tbsp cornstarch
1 tbsp soy sauce

¼ cup water
½ cup red pickled ginger sliced⎤
2 eggs   (p. 210)⎦
¾ cup flour
2 tbsp water
½ tsp salt

PREPARATION

1. Bring ¾ cup water to a boil. Add sugar and vinegar. Stir until the sugar is dissolved.

2. Combine cornstarch, soy sauce, and ¼ cup water. Add this to the vinegar-sugar mixture. Simmer over low heat, stirring constantly until the sauce thickens. Add ginger and set aside.

3. Bone the duck and, leaving the skin on the meat, cut it into cubes, 1½ inch to aside.

4. Lightly beat eggs; stir in flour, 2 tbsp water, and salt until batter is smooth.

5. Dip duck cubes in the batter and fry them in hot oil until they are golden brown. Drain the cubes on paper towels. Place them on a preheated serving plate. Reheat the sauce and pour over the fried duck.

Prawn Curry

(4 servings)

INGREDIENTS

1 lb fresh prawns
10 large firm tomatoes sliced
10 dried chilis pounded (40 are used in Malaya)
2 tbsp pounded duck or chicken meat
1 large onion sliced fine
1 2-inch piece of ginger chopped

1 tbsp curry powder
$\frac{1}{4}$ stem lemon grass
3 cups coconut milk
juice from 1 oz tamarind combined with hot water (lemon juice or puréed apricots)
1 tbsp butter
6 cloves garlic chopped

PREPARATION

1. Sauté the lemon grass, curry, and onion in 1 tbsp butter.

2. Shell and devein prawns, leaving tails on. Wash each prawn in salted water. Slit the backs, spread, and sprinkle with salt.

3. Mix the remainder of the ingredients with the onion mixture. Bring to a boil.

4. When the prawns change color, reduce heat and cook till liquid has evaporated.

Crab Rolls

(about 16 rolls)

INGREDIENTS

12 oz fresh or canned crab meat
12 oz harusame (vermicelli)
6 dried shiitake mushrooms
1 lb pork minced
1 cup chopped onion

4 egg yolks lightly beaten
1 tsp salt
$\frac{1}{2}$ tsp white pepper
1 tbsp vegetable oil
sugar

152

WRAPPERS

3 tbsp rice flour

1 tbsp wheat flour

4 egg whites beaten

½ cup water

a pinch of salt

cooking oil

SAUCE

6 tbsp anchovy paste

2 tbsp lemon juice

2 cloves garlic mashed

1 red chili pepper seeded and minced

1 green onion minced

PREPARATION

1. Mix flours. Gradually add water, three egg whites, and pinch of salt. Mix well. Brush a 6-inch skillet with oil, pour about 3 tbsp of batter into pan. Tip pan to coat bottom with a thin layer of batter. Cook until surface begins to bubble. Remove and set aside. Do not brown. The crêpes must be thin and white. Wrap in damp cloth to keep soft until needed.

2. In a deep bowl cover harusame noodles with 4 cups of water. In another bowl, combine mushrooms, 1 cup water, and a little sugar. Let soak for 30 minutes; then drain and discard water. Cut the noodles into 2-inch lengths. Cut off and discard mushroom stems and slice caps.

3. Thoroughly drain crab meat; remove small bits of bone.

4. In a round-bottom Chinese frying pan (wok)—or an ordinary skillet—heat 1 tbsp oil over moderate heat until a light haze forms above it. Sauté pork for 2 minutes. Transfer pork to a bowl. Sauté onions, crab meat, noodles, mushrooms, beaten egg yolks, salt and pepper. Combine with pork. In the center of each of the wrappers place 1 tbsp of this filling. Roll each into a cylinder about 4 inches long and 1 inch in diameter.

5. Place the filled rolls on a plate and cover with a towel. Refrigerate for 30 minutes before serving.

6. Make sauce by combining and mixing well the listed ingredients.

Chicken Noodle Soup

(6 servings)

INGREDIENTS

1 lb chicken breasts

2 oz harusame (or vermicelli)

4 dried shiitake mushrooms
6 cups chicken broth or stock
1 small onion minced
$\frac{1}{4}$ cup green onion minced
6 fresh coriander leaves or mint
  leaves chopped

1 tbsp vegetable oil
1 tbsp fish sauce or soy sauce
$\frac{1}{4}$ tsp white pepper
$\frac{1}{4}$ tsp monosodium glutamate

PREPARATION

1. Soak harusame noodles in 2 or 3 cups warm water for 30 minutes. Drain. Cut noodles into 2-inch lengths. Place the mushrooms in a small bowl and soak in water to cover for about 20 minutes. Cut off and discard stems. Slice caps crosswise into $\frac{1}{4}$-inch strips.

2. Put broth and chicken breasts in a pan and bring to boil over high heat. Skim off scum as it surfaces. Reduce heat to low. Cover and simmer for 8 to 10 minutes.

3. Skin and bone the chicken. Discard skin and bones. Cut meat into strips.

4. Heat oil in a skillet. Sauté onion for 1 minute. Add chicken and mushrooms. Stir for 1 minute.

5. Add onions, chicken, and mushrooms to soup and bring to a boil over high heat. Season with fish sauce and white pepper. Add noodles. Reduce heat to low and simmer for 5 minutes or until the noodles are tender.

6. Sprinkle with finely chopped green onions and coriander leaves. Serve at once.

Crab and Asparagus Soup

(4 servings)

INGREDIENTS

1 lb fresh or canned crab meat
2 tsp salt
$\frac{1}{2}$ lb fresh asparagus
4 cups chicken stock
1 medium onion sliced
1 tsp cornstarch mixed with
  $\frac{1}{2}$ cup of water

2 green onions cut into 1-inch
  lengths
4 dried shiitake mushrooms
$\frac{1}{4}$ tsp sugar
salt and pepper to taste

1. Soak dried mushrooms until soft in water with $\frac{1}{4}$ tsp sugar. Drain; reserve the water. Cut off and discard stems; slice caps into strips.

2. Wash asparagus and drain. Bring water to a boil over high heat. Add 2-tsp salt and asparagus. Parboil asparagus, drain, then rinse in cold running water. Dry thoroughly with paper towels. Cut into $1\frac{1}{2}$-inch lengths.

3. In a 4-quart saucepan, combine reserved mushroom water and chicken stock. Bring to a boil. Add onion slices. Reduce the heat to medium and simmer for 5 minutes or until onions are soft.

4. Add crab meat, asparagus, and mushrooms. Bring to a boil again. Stir cornstarch-and-water mixture into the soup. Stir constantly and gently. Simmer until the soup thickens and clears. Add salt and pepper to taste. Sprinkle with green onions and serve.

Taro-coconut-egg Custard

(4 servings)

INGREDIENTS

$\frac{1}{2}$ cup boiled, mashed
   taro root
3 eggs

$1\frac{1}{2}$ cups coconut milk
$\frac{1}{4}$ tsp salt
$\frac{1}{3}$ cup sugar

PREPARATION

1. Combine all ingredients, beat well, and strain into a greased baking dish or individual custard cups.

2. Place in pan of hot water and bake in preheated oven (300°) for 45 minutes to 1 hour or until set.

India

The daily lives of the Indian people are greatly influenced by religion, and certain diets are dictated by religious beliefs. Although India is the birthplace of Gautama Buddha, there are few followers of Buddhism today in the country; the majority are Hindus. The Hindu religion prohibits its adherents from eating beef because the cow is a sacred animal. Orthodox Hindus are strict vegetarians, who eat no fish, fowl, or even eggs. Mohammedans, of whom there are many in India, do not eat pork.

Because of the diversity of eating habits, Indian cuisine is complex, though representative dishes generally include the spice combination called curry. But here too great regional differences occur.

A well-prepared curry dish is one of the most delightful entrées one can serve. Throughout the Far East, curries are made with meat, poultry, seafood, eggs, and vegetables, though in the West, lamb, chicken, and seafood curries are best known.

Many Americans are unfamiliar with the subtle deliciousness of true Far Eastern curries for two reasons: they use inferior commercial curry powders instead of making their own, and they do not know the correct cooking procedures.

At parties many Indians serve mounds of crisp, wafer-thin pancakes called poppadams. They may be eaten alone, crumbled over rice, or as an accompaniment to rice and curry.

Other breadlike pancakes include chappattis, parrattas, and porrees. Chappattis and parrattas are about the size of a dinner plate. Chappattis are made of whole-wheat flour and little fat; parrattas, on the other hand, are often of white flour and call for more fat. Smaller porrees are cooked in fat or butter; they usually contain a filling. Chappattis and parrattas are eaten with curries, but not with rice.

Indians always eat with the fingers of the left hand. At the end of the meal, the hands are washed in finger bowls. Finally paan-daan, sometimes a plain metal box or a beautifully chased or filigreed silver casket, is served. The many small compartments of the box contain betel nut, saffron, cardamon, cloves, aniseed, and many other spices which are eaten with betel leaves, sometimes covered with silver leaf.

Skewered Beef Curry or Hussainee Beef Curry

(4-6 servings)

INGREDIENTS

2 lb beef
1½ tbsp butter
½ tsp salt
4 tsp grated onion
1 tsp turmeric
½ tsp ground ginger
½ cup water

¼ tsp garlic powder
½ tsp chili powder
1½-inch slice of fresh ginger root grated
2 or 3 small onions finely sliced
1 cup yogurt
6 metal skewers

PREPARATION

1. Cut the beef into 1-inch cubes. Skewer the slices of onion with beef until all six skewers are filled.

2. Heat butter in a pan then add remaining ingredients, spices, and half cup of water. Cook till the mixture browns; stir while cooking.

3. Add the six filled skewers and the yogurt. Coat the meat well with the spice and yogurt mixture.

4. Tightly cover and simmer over very low heat for 2 hours or until the meat is tender. Serve on skewers in a large warm dish. This dish is delicious with parrattas or chappattis (see p. 165).

Rich Indian Curried Steaks

(4-6 servings)

INGREDIENTS

2 lbs beef sliced for steaks
1½ inches fresh ginger chopped
2 green chilis chopped
2 onions chopped

1 pint water
¼ lb butter (or mustard oil)
1 tbsp vinegar
½ tsp salt

1. Mix ginger, chilis, onion, and salt. Coat each slice of meat with some of this mixture. Combine coated meat, water, butter, and vinegar in a heavy pan. Cover tightly and bring to a boil.

2. Simmer till the water has evaporated; stir the meat gently and fry five minutes. No liquid will remain after the frying.

Curry Fricassee

(4-6 servings)

INGREDIENTS

$\frac{1}{2}$ lb sliced cooked cold mutton or beef
2 cups freshly cooked mashed potatoes
2 tbsp butter (or mustard oil)
3 onions sliced

$\frac{1}{2}$ tsp ground red chili
5 cloves garlic mashed
$\frac{1}{2}$ tsp salt
$\frac{1}{2}$ cup stock mixed with 2 tbsp vinegar
chopped parsley and mint

PREPARATION

1. Put the butter into a heavy pan and heat till smoke rises. Drop in the onion and sauté till light brown. Add chili, salt, and garlic and sauté for five minutes over a brisk flame, stirring constantly.

2. Add meat and stock, mix thoroughly, and simmer for ten minutes.

3. Mix mashed potatoes with parsley and mint and mold into a ring. Pour the curry in the center of the ring. Serve hot.

Pork Curry

(6-8 servings)

INGREDIENTS

2 lb pork or beef
6 oz mustard oil
1 large garlic clove mashed
1 tsp ground ginger
1 tsp ground coriander
$\frac{1}{2}$ tsp ground cumin
2 or 3 bay leaves

12 peppercorns
6 ground cloves
5 ground cardamons
6 small sticks of cinnamon (2 inches each) ground
1 tbsp vinegar
$\frac{1}{2}$ tsp salt

PREPARATION

1. The tastiest curry is cooked in mustard oil. Cut pork into large cubes.

2. Thoroughly mix vinegar, all the ground spices, and ½ tsp salt. Marinate the pork in this mixture for 18-24 hours. Treated in this way the meat will keep for two or three days without danger of spoiling.

3. Heat the mustard oil in a heavy pan, add meat, spices, vinegar, peppercorns, and bay leaves. Simmer gently over a low heat for two hours until the meat is tender; serve hot.

Mutton Curry

(4-6 servings)

INGREDIENTS

1 lb mutton or lamb cut into small pieces
1 tbsp butter
1 large onion sliced
2 cloves garlic chopped
2 tsp ground cumin seed
1 tsp ground mustard seed

½ tsp ground red chili
¾ tsp ground saffron or turmeric
¾ cup of stock
½ tsp salt
1 tsp brown sugar
1 tsp vinegar

PREPARATION

1. Fry onion till golden in the butter. Add garlic and spices and heat well. Then add the mutton and sauté briefly.

2. Now add ¾ cup of stock, salt, and sugar. Cover and simmer for 25 minutes. Before serving, add 1 tsp vinegar. Serve hot.

Chicken Curry

(4-6 servings)

INGREDIENTS

1 chicken cut into serving pieces
5 oz butter (preferably ghee; see p. 199)

1 cup yogurt
4 tsp sliced onions
1 tsp ground chili

1 tsp coriander seed
6 small sticks cinnamon (about
   1 inch long) ground
3 blades of lemon grass (or
   1 tbsp grated lemon rind)
½ tsp ground ginger
1 tsp salt
2 cloves of garlic mashed

10 peppercorns
5 cloves
6 ground cardamons
3 bay leaves
½ pint water or stock
juice of 1 lemon
12 large onions sliced lengthwise

PREPARATION

1. Heat the butter or ghee, sauté the sliced onions till golden brown, and set aside. Then sauté garlic and all spices except bay leaves and lemon grass. Add the pieces of chicken and salt. Sauté till brown.

2. Add yogurt, bay leaves, lemon grass, stock, and fried onions. Bring to a boil, cover closely, and simmer for 1½–2 hours till chicken is tender.

3. Remove from heat, pour in lemon juice, mix, remove lemon grass, and serve with steamed rice.

Duck Pot Roast with Spicy Cabbage

(8 servings)

INGREDIENTS

1 plump duck
1 cabbage cut into quarters
1 tsp ground saffron or turmeric
1 pint water
1½ tsp salt
6 large onions cut into halves

1 tbsp butter
3 green chilis cut lengthwise
   into quarters
6 cloves garlic chopped
1½ inches fresh ginger sliced thin
½ cup vinegar

PREPARATION

1. Use a large, deep saucepan. Place the cabbage on the bottom, (if you wish, cut it into smaller pieces). Put in the whole duck.

2. Mix saffron or turmeric and salt with water and pour the mixture over the duck.

3. Add onions, chili, fresh ginger, garlic, and butter.

4. Bring to a boil; simmer for 1 hour or until the duck is done. Five minutes before serving, add vinegar. Serve hot.

160

Lamb Curry

(6 servings)

INGREDIENTS

2 lb lamb (or one roasting chicken jointed)
½ lb washed lentils
3 onions cut into pieces
2 large potatoes cut into pieces
4 tomatoes
1 eggplant
2 oz fat
lemon juice

3 tsp salt
½ tsp ground red chili
½ tsp ground coriander
pinch ground cinnamon
½ tsp ground turmeric
½ tsp ground cumin
pinch ground cloves
2 green chilis
3 sprigs fresh mint

PREPARATION

1. Place meat and lentils in 2 pints boiling water. Add potatoes, tomatoes, onions, and egg plant. Simmer until meat is tender.

2. Remove meat, strain the liquid, and discard the residue.

3. Return meat to the strained liquid, add red chili, coriander, cinnamon, turmeric, cummin, cloves, mint, green chilis, 2 oz fat, lemon juice, and salt. Cook for 15 minutes. Total cooking time is about 2 hours.

Fried Minced Meat

(4 servings)

INGREDIENTS

1 lb minced meat
2 small onions diced
½ cup split peas
4 cloves garlic

4 cardamons
8 black peppercorns
1 egg well beaten
salt and pepper to taste

PREPARATION

1. This dish is in fact Pakistani in origin. Place all the ingredients except the egg, in a large skillet. Cover with water and simmer gently till the liquid has evaporated. The mixture must be thick and the meat tender.

2. Mix in one beaten egg. Pass the mixture through a food chopper

and allow to cool. Finally mold the mixture into small cubes and deep-fat fry till brown.

Curried Cauliflower and Peas

INGREDIENTS

1 large head cauliflower (2½ lb)	¾ tsp ground cumin
1 cup peas	¼ tsp ground black pepper
½ cup onions chopped	3 tbsp butter
4 tsp ground coriander	2¼ tsp salt
1 tsp ground turmeric	1 bay leaf

PREPARATION

1. Blend coriander, turmeric, cumin, and black pepper with 3 tbsp water.

2. In a medium skillet, heat butter until bubbling. Sauté the spice mixture in hot butter over low heat, stirring constantly for 2 minutes.

3. Add cauliflower broken into flowerets, onions, peas, salt, and bay leaf. Mix thoroughly. Add ¼ cup water. Cook until the cauliflower is tender (about 10 to 15 minutes).

Indian Cabbage

(4 servings)

INGREDIENTS

1 small head cabbage chopped fine	2 green chilis
	2 oz oil or butter
2 onions chopped fine	¼ tsp ground turmeric
1 tsp salt	½ tsp whole mustard seeds
2 tomatoes cut into pieces	¼ tsp monosodium glutamate

PREPARATION

1. Heat cooking oil or butter. Add mustard seeds and sauté till seeds pop open. Add onions and tomatoes. Sauté for 10 minutes then add cabbage, chilis, and turmeric. Cook till cabbage is tender.

2. Add salt and monosodium glutamate to taste.

Yogurt, Cucumber, and Potato Salad

(4-6 servings)

INGREDIENTS

2 medium cucumbers
2 medium tomatoes
1 medium potato
2 cups yogurt

salt and pepper to taste
paprika
monosodium glutamate
¼ tsp cumin

PREPARATION

1. Drop the potato into enough boiling water to cover and boil briskly uncovered until tender. Drain, peel, and cut into ½-inch cubes.

2. Partially peel cucumber and slice it lengthwise into halves. Scoop out the seeds by running the tip of a teaspoon down the center of each half. Cut the cucumber lengthwise into ¼-inch pieces.

3. Cut tomatoes crosswise into ½-inch rounds, slice into ½-inch strips and then into ½-inch cubes.

4. Combine the cucumber, tomato, and salt in a small bowl and mix thoroughly. Let the mixture rest at room temperature for 3-5 minutes then drain off excess liquid.

5. In a salad bowl, combine potato, tomatoes, and cucumbers. Toss together gently but thoroughly. Combine yogurt, salt and pepper to taste, monosodium glutamate, and cumin. Pour sauce over vegetables turning them with a spoon to coat evenly. Correct seasoning, cover tightly, and chill at least 1 hour before serving. Sprinkle with paprika before serving.

Pineapple Chutney

(3 pints)

INGREDIENTS

1 cup red wine
1 cup vinegar
1 cup packed brown sugar
6 cups drained fresh or canned
  pineapple chunks
1 cup sliced blanched almonds

¾ cup light raisins
1½ tsp fresh ginger grated
1½ tsp salt
¾ tsp cayenne pepper
½ tsp garlic minced
¼ tsp ground cloves

PREPARATION

1. Combine red wine, vinegar, and brown sugar. Mix well. Then add pineapple, almonds, raisins, ginger, salt, cayenne pepper, garlic, and cloves.

2. In a large saucepan, bring mixture to a boil, stirring constantly. Simmer until mixture thickens.

3. Pour immediately into sterilized jars and seal. Store in refrigerator.

Apricot Chutney

(approximately 3 pints)

INGREDIENTS

2½ lbs apricots pitted and quartered
2 cups light raisins chopped
1 lb red onions peeled and coarsely diced
1 lb dark brown sugar

2 cups vinegar
½ tsp cinnamon
1 tsp chili powder
2 tsp mustard seed
1 tsp salt
1 tsp turmeric

PREPARATION

1. Boil apricots and sugar until the mixture is the consistency of jam.

2. Combine all ingredients in a large pot and simmer uncovered over low heat for 1 hour or until the juice has thickened. Cool and pour into sterilized jars cover and seal.

Sweet Lime Chutney

INGREDIENTS

25 limes or lemons
4 tsp salt
1 cup vinegar
¼ lb raisins
¼ lb chopped dates

1½ inches fresh ginger sliced thin
3 to 4 cloves garlic mashed
3 or 4 red chilis
1½ tsp mustard seed
½ cup brown sugar

PREPARATION

1. Cut the limes (or lemons) into quarters but do not separate the

pieces. Rub the flesh with salt and expose the fruit to the sun for three days, turning daily. Heat them in a slow oven until the fruit is well dried.

2. Seed and grind the limes with vinegar and remaining ingredients.

3. Bring to a boil then simmer for 30 minutes.
Let stand to cool.

4. Pour into sterile jars. Refrigerate and use as needed.

Fresh Coriander Chutney

(1 cup)

INGREDIENTS

¼ cup grated coconut (fresh coconut is preferred)

1 onion coarsely chopped

2 cups coriander leaves and stems, chopped

6 black peppercorns

juice of 2 lemons

1 tbsp fresh ginger peeled and chopped

¼ tsp fresh chili pepper

PREPARATION

1. In an electric blender, combine all of the ingredients except the chili pepper.

2. When the mixture is smooth, add the chili pepper, blend and season to taste. Add more chili if desired.

Indian Bread (Chappatti)

Until the advent of the British, bread made with yeast was virtually unknown in India. For people with sound teeth (or well designed dentures), unleavened bread is both more nutritious and tastier than commercially produced bread. British people who have made its acquaintance in India like the local bread, but it is rarely seen in English homes. English wives seem to think that some mystery surrounds its production when, in fact, it is much easier to make than yeast-risen bread.

INGREDIENTS

1 lb whole-wheat flour

1 cup water

salt

PREPARATION

1. Mix the flour with water and a pinch of salt to make a fairly stiff dough.

2. Knead well. Pinch off pieces of the dough and mold them into balls the size of a walnut.

3. Roll each ball in flour. Flour the pastry board. Roll each ball into a thin pancake.

4. Heat a large unoiled frying pan. Fry each pancake for 2 minutes to a side.

5. After frying them all, coat each side of each chappatti with butter, return them to the frying pan, and fry to a light brown color. Eat while hot either plain or with curry dishes.

Carrot Halvah

(6 servings)

INGREDIENTS

2 cups grated carrots
1 cup cooking oil or butter
1 can (14 oz) sweetened
  condensed milk
1 can (14 oz) water

2 tbsp blanched almonds
  chopped
2 tbsp raisins chopped
$\frac{1}{4}$ tsp ground saffron
1 tbsp fresh lime juice heated

PREPARATION

1. Combine 1 can of water with condensed milk and bring to a boil. Add carrots and cook over low heat for about 45 minutes, stirring occasionally.

2. Add oil or butter gradually. Then add almonds, raisins, and saffron dissolved in lime juice. Eat either hot or cold.

Iran

Agriculture is the prime industry of Iran; and large quantities of wheat, barley, rice, sugar beets, and tobacco are grown on the plateaus of the land. The orchards yield a great variety of fruits: pomegranates, cherries, plums, grapes, melons of all kinds, peaches, figs, and dates. Nuts grow in profusion especially pistachios, hazelnuts, and almonds.

Mutton and lamb are preferred to other meats, though venison and veal are also popular. Since Iran is a Mohammedan nation, pork and wines are forbidden, but some Iranians do drink small quantities of liquors at parties and on special occasions.

Iranian food represents the cuisine of most of the Arabic-speaking countries. The same dishes appear on tables all through the Middle East, but their origin is deeply rooted in the culinary history of Iran. Iranian curries are mildly spiced. Turmeric and saffron are used in many dishes, as are cardamon, cinnamon, and clove.

The cuisine of the Iranians has much in common with all Eastern foods but, like Turkish cookery, uses fewer pungent spices than the dishes of India, Pakistan, Ceylon, Burma, Indonesia, and Malaya.

Skewered Lamb Iranian Style

(4 servings)

INGREDIENTS

1 lb leg of young lamb
½ tsp ground cinnamon
½ tsp black pepper
6 to 10 cloves of garlic mashed
1 tsp ground coriander
1 tbsp butter
¼ tsp nutmeg

6 tomatoes sliced
2 onions sliced
1 cup fine rice
1 cup stock or water
salt to taste
metal skewers
parsley

167

1. Wash 1 cup of rice twice in water and place it in a bowl. Cover with water. Put into the bowl $\frac{1}{2}$ tsp of salt in a cotton or muslin bag—it is important that the salt does not touch the rice. Leave for 24 hours. Drain in a colander.

2. Fry drained rice in butter till golden brown. Add 1 cup of stock or water and bring to a boil. Lower heat till the contents simmer. Cover closely and cook till the water has evaporated entirely. The rice should be thoroughly cooked: the grains must not stick together. If rice is not done, add a little more water and cook till it evaporates.

3. Cut the lamb into $1\frac{1}{2}$-inch cubes. Mix the ground spices in a little tomato juice to make a paste. Rub this well into the meat. Allow the lamb to marinate for 1 hour.

4. Skewer the lamb: a piece of lamb, a slice of onion, and finally a slice of tomato, then another piece of lamb, and so on.

5. Grill the skewered lamb over a charcoal fire or under a gas or electric grill till tender. Turn the skewers from time to time so that the lamb cooks evenly on all sides.

6. Serve with rice and onion, nuts, and parsley garnishes.

Lentil Soup

(6 servings)

INGREDIENTS

1 lb brisket of lamb	$\frac{1}{2}$ cup lime juice
2 cups lentils	6 cups hot water
1 large onion chopped	1 tsp salt
$\frac{1}{2}$ small head cabbage chopped	1 green onion chopped
$\frac{1}{2}$ tsp turmeric	6 radishes
$\frac{1}{2}$ tsp pepper	mint leaves

PREPARATION

1. Put meat and lentils into a deep kettle. Add onion, turmeric, pepper, lime juice, and hot water. Cover tightly and cook over low heat for 1 hour.

2. Add cabbage and salt. Cover and simmer for 1 hour or until meat is very tender. Add water if needed.

3. Strain off liquid, which is served separately as an accompaniment to the meat. Discard bones. Pound meat and remaining ingredients with a potato masher to form a smooth paste. You may use an electric blender at high speed.

4. Shape purée into a mound on serving dish and sprinkle with green onions, decoratively trimmed radishes, and mint leaves. Serve with the reserved lentil stock.

Mixed Nuts

INGREDIENTS

shelled pistachios
almonds
hazelnuts
pumpkin seeds

watermelon seeds
salt
lime juice

PREPARATION

1. Mix the nuts, salt them, and allow them to marinate covered tightly 10 minutes in a mixture of equal parts of lime juice and water.

2. Drain and toast briefly in a hot oven.

Minced Meat

(4 serving)

INGREDIENTS

1 large onion chopped
4 tbsp butter
1 lb ground lamb or beef
½ tsp pepper
½ tsp turmeric
1 cup tomato juice
¾ cup hot water

½ cup dried yellow split peas
¼ cup lime juice
½ tsp salt
½ pound pitted sour cherries
 or 1 cup diced tart apples
¼ tsp saffron

PREPARATION

1. Sauté onion in butter until golden. Remove and drain on a paper towel. Stir-sauté meat with pepper and turmeric in remaining butter until brown. Add tomato juice and hot water, cover, and simmer over

medium heat until meat is tender.

2. Add split peas, lime juice, and salt. Cover lightly and simmer over low heat for 45 minutes.

3. Add fried onion and cherries or apples and continue to cook until all ingredients are done and a rich gravy forms.

4. Pour into a heated serving bowl and sprinkle with saffron mixed with a little hot water.

Minced Duck and Walnuts

(4 servings)

INGREDIENTS

1 large onion minced
½ tsp pepper
½ tsp turmeric
2 tbsp butter
1 lb diced meat from a small
  duck (discard fat and skin)
2 tbsp flour
½ lb walnut meats coarsely
  chopped

⅓ cup hot water
1½ cup pomegranate or
  cranberry juice
salt
juice of 1 or 2 lemons
1 small eggplant
cooking oil
1½ tsp cardamon powder

PREPARATION

1. Sauté onion, pepper, and turmeric in butter until well browned. Drain onion on paper towel. In remaining butter sauté duck meat until browned.

2. Sprinkle duck with flour, add walnuts, and sauté a few more minutes. Add water, pomegranate or cranberry juice, and salt. Add lemon juice (this dish must be sour), cover, and simmer over low heat for 30 minutes.

3. Peel eggplant, cut lengthwise into sixths, and sprinkle with salt. Stack pieces and drain. Rinse in cold water, dry, and sauté in hot oil until lightly browned on all sides. Place eggplant on meat, add sautéed onion, cover lightly and simmer over low heat until eggplant is tender and a rich gravy forms.

4. Gradually stir in cardamon and cook for about 5 minutes.

Eggplant and Chicken Casserole

(8 servings)

INGREDIENTS

2 large eggplants
2 large onions sliced
1 large chicken cut into serving
   pieces
4 tomatoes peeled and chopped
   or a 1 large can of tomatoes

½ green pepper cut into rings
juice of 2 lemons
2 tsp salt
¼ tsp pepper
1 cup cooking oil
½ tsp saffron

PREPARATION

1. Peel and slice eggplant. Sprinkle with salt and stack to drain.

2. In a deep pot or casserole arrange layers of onion slices, green pepper slices, chicken, and chopped tomatoes. Add a layer of tomatoes last. Sprinkle with lemon juice, salt and pepper. Cover tightly and simmer over low heat for 1 hour. Gently stir to mix all ingredients.

3. Rinse and dry eggplant and sauté until browned on both sides.

4. Arrange eggplant on top of meat and vegetables, partially cover, and cook over moderate heat for 15 to 20 minutes or until gravy is reduced to a rich glaze. Mix saffron with a little hot water and sprinkle on ingredients. Serve in the casserole in which it was cooked.

Leaf Kabab

(6 servings)

INGREDIENTS

2 lb beef fillet or top round
4 large onions minced
1 cup lemon juice

salt
pepper

PREPARATION

1. Cut meat into thin slices about 3 inches wide and 4 inches long. Pound each slice gently with sharp edge of a knife to make fine cuts in the meat. Do not cut all the way through. Place meat in a pottery or glass bowl.

2. Mince 4 large onions and cover the meat with them.

3. Add 1 cup of lemon juice and refrigerate for 2 or 3 days. About

20 minutes before serving, remove meat. Discard onion. Sprinkle meat with salt and pepper.

4. Insert 2 skewers in each piece of meat, pierce from one side then the other to keep pieces flat. Broil under broiler or over charcoal, turning several times until meat is browned on all sides. It must be juicy and not overcooked.

Buttered Rice

(6-8 servings)

INGREDIENTS

1 lb long-grain rice
2 tbsp butter
3 tbsp salt
1 tbsp water

$\frac{1}{3}$ cup milk
3 tbsp melted butter
2 tbsp hot water

PREPARATION

1. Wash rice and fill a 4-quart saucepan with water. Bring to a rapid boil. Add rice and salt and boil for 10 minutes uncovered. Drain and rinse with lukewarm water.

2. In casserole heat 2 tbsp butter and 1 tbsp water. When butter melts, swirl to spread buttery liquid evenly over the bottom.

3. Mix $\frac{1}{2}$ cup cooked rice and milk and spread in bottom of casserole. Fill with remaining rice, mounding in center. Make a small, deep hole in center. Bake in 375° oven for 15 minutes.

4. Remove cover and sprinkle rice with additional melted butter mixed with 2 tbsp hot water. Reduce heat to 350°. Cover casserole and bake for 30 minutes.

5. Remove casserole from oven and place on cool surface for 19 minutes. Stir rice gently. Turn it out on a heated serving dish a brown crust should have formed on the bottom. This crust must be on top when the dish is served.

Peach Pickles

(about 3 8-ounce jars)

INGREDIENTS

1 lb dried peaches or apricots

1 tbsp minced ginger root

172

4 cups vinegar

2 tbsp coriander seeds lightly toasted

1 whole bulb garlic peeled

$\frac{1}{4}$ lb dried tamarind pods

$\frac{1}{2}$ tsp red pepper

$\frac{1}{2}$ cup sugar

1 tsp salt

1 tsp black pepper

PREPARATION

1. Soak peaches and ginger root in 3 cups vinegar at least 2 hours, or overnight.

2. Put fruit and vinegar in a kettle and add coriander and garlic.

3. Soak tamarinds in remaining cup of vinegar and rub between fingers until all the pulp is dissolved and smooth. Strain liquid into other ingredients.

4. Add remaining ingredients. Bring to a boil and simmer for 15 minutes or until thick. Pour into sterile jars and seal.

Cucumber Salad

INGREDIENTS

2 small seeded cucumbers

1 cup yogurt

3 tbsp white raisins

$\frac{1}{4}$ cup chopped walnuts

1 small onion minced

salt

pepper

powdered mint to taste

PREPARATION

1. Peel and coarsely grate 2 small seeded cucumbers. Mix with 1 cup yogurt.

2. Add remaining ingredients and chill thoroughly before serving.

The Levant

In this group of recipes I have included representative examples of the cuisines of Syria, Turkey, and Greece. Seafoods and unexcelled ways of preparing lamb are specialties of the region, and no one who has tasted authentic Turkish pastry can forget it. The preparation of the pastry itself, and of the phylo pastry used in Greek cooking, is so difficult that many Middle-Eastern housewives do not attempt it themselves but purchase it ready made. Most foodstores stocking Middle-Eastern foods carry it.

You will notice that there are several recipes calling for eggplant. In the United States, the usual way to serve this vegetable is breaded and fried. I feel certain that once you have tried it in some of the more interesting Levantine ways, you will prefer them. Yogurt, too, occurs in many recipes of this region. And this is good since it is both delicious and nutritious. I have given several Levantine bread recipes, which I recommend that you try for variety. Remember that most of these breads contain no oil and therefore dry out rapidly.

Syria

Baked Fish with Sesame-oil Sauce

(6 servings)

INGREDIENTS

3 lb fish
1½ cups onion chopped or
   sliced
¼ cup lemon juice

1 cup sesame oil
¼ cup water
1 tsp salt
olive oil

PREPARATION

1. Clean the fish. Rub it with olive oil, sprinkle it with salt, and bake it in a 350° oven for about 35 minutes or until flesh flakes easily.

2. Sauté onion in oil until golden.

3. To make sesame-oil sauce beat lemon juice and water into sesame oil. Put sauce ingredients into blender, cover, and blend until smooth and milky. Mix the onions in the sauce, pour over baked fish, and continue to bake for about 20 minutes. Chill before serving.

Stuffed Squash

(6 servings)

INGREDIENTS

1½ lb ground lamb or beef
12 small summer squash
1 cup rice washed and drained
2 tbsp melted butter

1 large clove garlic minced
1 tsp dried mint
1 6-oz can tomato paste
1 tsp salt and pepper

PREPARATION

1. Peel squash and remove seeds by making a hole about ½ inch in diameter all the way through the squash.

2. Combine rice and lamb with melted butter and salt and pepper to

taste and mix well. Stuff the squash with this mixture, leaving one inch open at each end to allow filling to expand.

3. Heat oil in a saucepan and sauté garlic until golden. Set aside. Arrange the squash in a pot and sprinkle with garlic and mint. Mix tomato paste with water and pour over the squash.

4. Bring liquid to a boil and simmer over low heat for about 40 minutes or until squash is tender.

Stewed Okra

(6 servings)

INGREDIENTS

3 cups young okra
10 tiny white onions
3 medium tomatoes sliced
8 cloves garlic
½ cup lemon juice
4½ cups cold water

½ tsp sugar
½ tsp pepper
3 tsp salt
4 tbsp vegetable oil
1 tsp coriander seeds
½ tsp monosodium glutamate

PREPARATION

1. Cut the stems from the okra, wash well, and drain in a colander. Bring 4 cups water to a boil over high heat. Add 2 tsp salt and the okra; parboil to preserve green color. Plunge into cold water and pat dry with paper towels.

2. Crush together garlic, dash of salt, and coriander seeds.

3. Heat oil in a skillet over a moderate heat until a light haze forms over it. Sprinkle 1 tsp salt over the okra and sauté until tender. Remove and set aside. Fry onions until golden brown. Combine with the okra. In 1 tbsp oil sauté the garlic-coriander mixture for about 1 minute.

4. Make a layer of sliced tomatoes in a deep pan and cover it with okra. Make a depression in the center and fill with onions. Sprinkle with garlic-coriander mixture and add lemon juice, water, sugar, and pepper. Bring to a boil, cover, and simmer for 10 minutes.

5. Uncover and simmer until liquid evaporates. Sprinkle with monosodium glutamate and correct seasoning. Chill. This colorful dish is served as an appetizer before the meal.

Eggplant with Yogurt

(2 servings)

INGREDIENTS

1 large eggplant
1 clove garlic minced
1 cup yogurt

1 tsp salt
olive oil for frying
½ tsp monosodium glutamate

PREPARATION

1. Peel eggplant and slice thin. Sprinkle slices of eggplant with salt and stack one on top of the other. Set aside for about 1 hour. Rinse with cold water and dry with paper towels.

2. Sauté eggplant slices on both sides in olive oil until tender and golden.

3. Put into a mixing bowl and blend with garlic, salt, and yogurt. Sprinkle with monosodium glutamate. Chill and serve as an appetizer.

Arab Bread

(8 loaves)

INGREDIENTS

5 to 6 cups enriched flour
½ cup yellow corn meal
1 pkg active dry yeast (2 tsp)

2 cups lukewarm water
2 tsp salt
1 tbsp oil

PREPARATION

1. Soften yeast in lukewarm water. Stir in salt and oil. Gradually beat in enough flour to make a dough that does not stick to the hands.

2. Turn out on a floured board and knead until smooth. Brush surface of dough with oil, cover with a towel and let rise in a warm place until double in bulk (about 2 hours).

3. Punch down and cut into 8 equal pieces. Knead each piece until dough is very smooth. Brush each ball with oil, cover and let rise for 30 minutes.

4. Mix corn meal with ½ cup flour. Roll each ball of dough in the mixture and flatten with the palm of the hand to the size of a pancake. Set each aside and keep covered with a towel.

5. Roll each piece as thin as possible.

6. Place on a greased cookie sheet and bake one at a time in a pre-heated 450° oven for 5 minutes or until the bottom is lightly browned.

7. Remove from oven and place in the broiler for 15 seconds or until the top is browned. Like most Arab breads, this version dries out quickly because it contains no milk and little shortening.

Vegetable Soup

(6 servings)

INGREDIENTS

1 lb beef (with bone)
½ head cabbage shredded
3 carrots skinned and diced
2 stalks celery sliced
1 large can whole tomatoes (2 cups)

1 medium onion diced
1 clove garlic minced
¼ cup parsley minced
¼ tsp pepper
3 quarts water
1 tsp salt

PREPARATION

1. Wash beef, soak briefly to remove blood and deodorize, then put in a large soup kettle. Add 2 quarts water and salt. Bring to a boil and remove the scum that floats to the surface.

2. Reduce heat and simmer covered for 3 hours. When the broth comes to a boil add 1 cup of water. Repeat this 4 times to keep the soup clear.

3. Add remaining ingredients except the parsley. Cover and continue to simmer for 30 minutes. Season to taste with salt and pepper. Serve hot garnished with minced parsley.

Mixed Salad

(6 servings)

INGREDIENTS

1 large cucumber peeled and diced
4 ripe tomatoes peeled, seeded, and chopped

1 green pepper seeded and chopped

1 bunch radishes sliced
1 bunch green onions sliced
1 bunch parsley chopped
2 cups romaine shredded
1 tbsp shredded fresh mint

1 clove garlic minced
2 tbsp lemon juice
⅓ cup olive oil
salt and pepper to taste

PREPARATION

1. Prepare the vegetables and combine in a salad bowl.

2. Sprinkle with salt and pepper. Add lemon juice and olive oil. Toss lightly and serve.

Pickled Cauliflower

(4 servings)

INGREDIENTS

1 large cauliflower
4 tsp salt
1 tbsp all-purpose flour
1 cup milk
4 cups water

1 cup vinegar
2 small peeled beets
cheesecloth
2 pickle jars

PREPARATION

1. Wash a large head of cauliflower and remove the leaves. Parboil in 2 cups salted water (2 tsp salt is added) to which has been added 1 cup milk and flour. Spread cheesecloth over top of pan, cover, and cook till cauliflower is almost tender.

2. Combine 2 cups water, 1 cup vinegar, and 2 tsp salt.

3. Pack cauliflower into clean jars, cover with vinegar solution, and add 1 peeled beet for color. Cover tightly and let stand in refrigerator for 1 week before serving.

Pickled Mushrooms

(2 pints)

INGREDIENTS

2 lb small mushrooms
1 pint vinegar
½ tbsp salt
juice of one lemon

1½ tbsp peppercorns cracked
½ cup olive oil
¼ tsp oregano or thyme
2 pint jars

1. Wipe mushrooms with a paper towel and cut off the tough ends of the stems. Do not peel. Use only small, firm mushrooms.

2. Place mushrooms in a saucepan with salt, lemon juice and water to cover. Bring to a boil and simmer for 5 minutes. Drain and dry.

3. Pack mushrooms in clean pint jars and sprinkle with cracked peppercorns.

4. In an enamel saucepan (not an aluminum one), combine vinegar, olive oil, and oregano or thyme. Bring to a boil. Pour hot vinegar mixture over mushrooms and seal at once. Store for at least one week before serving.

Turkey

Stuffed Eggplant

(6 servings)

INGREDIENTS

3 medium eggplants cut into $\frac{1}{2}$-inch slices

4 tbsp butter

2 medium onions chopped (1 cup)

2 cloves garlic minced

$\frac{1}{2}$ cup olive oil

1 cup chopped mushrooms

2 lbs ground cooked lamb

3 tbsp tomato paste

2 tbsp parsley chopped

2 tsp salt

$\frac{1}{2}$ tsp pepper

$\frac{1}{2}$ tsp nutmeg

$\frac{1}{8}$ tsp basil

3 eggs lightly beaten

$\frac{1}{2}$ cup bread crumbs

$\frac{1}{2}$ cup grated parmesan cheese

1 lemon sliced

1 tomato

PREPARATION

1. Soak eggplant in salt water for an hour or more. Dry with paper towels. Spread eggplant slices in large roasting pan. Sprinkle with $\frac{1}{4}$ cup olive oil. Cover with foil and bake in 350° oven 30 minutes. Remove and keep warm.

2. Heat butter in a large skillet and sauté onion and garlic until onions are transparent. Add remaining $\frac{1}{4}$ cup olive oil and mushrooms, ground lamb, tomato paste, parsley, salt, pepper, nutmeg, and basil. Mix well; cook over moderate heat for 5 minutes. Stir occasionally. Remove from heat and stir in eggs.

3. Grease the bottom and sides of a charlotte mold or bowl 7 inches in diameter and 4 inches high and sprinkle the bottom with bread crumbs. Cover with a layer of eggplant, then a layer of lamb mixture; repeat until both mixtures are used up. Sprinkle with cheese.

4. Place mold in a large pan containing 1 inch of hot water and bake in a preheated oven at 375° for 50-60 minutes. Remove from oven, let stand 2 minutes, then unmold on heated serving platter.

5. Top with tomato sauce and decorate with lemon slices and tomato wedges.

Stuffed Mussels

(6 servings)

INGREDIENTS

18 large mussels
1 cup liquid drained from
   mussels
$\frac{1}{2}$ cup rice washed and drained
4 tbsp olive oil
1 cup water
2 large onions minced

2 tbsp pine nuts
2 tbsp currants
1 tbsp chopped parsley
$\frac{1}{4}$ tsp allspice
$\frac{1}{4}$ tsp pepper
$\frac{1}{2}$ tsp salt
lemon wedges

PREPARATION

1. Soak mussels in salted water for 1 hour. Scrape shells thoroughly.

2. Place mussels in a saucepan with 1 cup of water. Cover tightly, bring to a boil and cook 2 to 3 minutes or until mussels have opened. Discard any that do not open.

3. Heat oil in a skillet and cook onion until soft; do not allow to brown. Add rice, cover, and cook over low heat for 10 minutes.

4. Add liquid from mussels and remaining ingredients. Mix lightly, cover, and cook over low heat for from 15 to 20 minutes or until the rice is done.

5. Remove mussels from shells and add to rice. Fill mussel shells with the mixture and serve either hot or cold garnished with lemon wedges.

Yogurt Soup

(4 servings)

INGREDIENTS

$\frac{1}{2}$ cup pearl barley
4 cups chicken broth
2 cups yogurt at room
   temperature

2 large onions chopped
2 tbsp butter

½ cup fresh mint or 1 tsp mint
flakes
1 tsp salt

⅛ tsp white pepper
¼ tsp monosodium glutamate
few sprigs of parsley

PREPARATION

1. Soak barley overnight in water to cover. Drain and cook with chicken broth for about 15 minutes or until tender.

2. Heat butter in a skillet over moderate heat until a light haze forms over it. Sauté onion till transparent. Add it to the broth. Add mint, parsley, salt, and pepper to taste. Simmer for 30 minutes.

3. Five minutes before serving, remove from heat. Let stand 3 minutes, and stir in yogurt mixed with a little hot broth.

Cracked-wheat Pilaf

(6 servings)

INGREDIENTS

2 cups cracked wheat
4 cups chicken stock
1 medium onion chopped

½ cup butter
1 tsp salt
pepper

PREPARATION

1. Heat butter in a skillet. Sauté onion until soft and yellow but not brown. Add cracked wheat, mix well, cover, and cook over low heat for 10 minutes.

2. Combine this with chicken stock and salt and pepper to taste. Put in a casserole and cover. Bake in a preheated 350° oven for 30 minutes. Stir gently with a fork and continue to bake for 15 minutes or until all the liquid is absorbed and the cracked wheat is moist and fluffy.

Rice Pudding

(6 servings)

INGREDIENTS

¾ cup pulverized rice
¾ cup water or ½ cup fresh
orange juice and ¼ cup water
2 cups milk

¾ cup sugar
1 tsp orange juice
chopped pistachio nuts

1. Pound raw rice in a bowl or blend at high speed in an electric blender until pulverized. Mix rice with water.

2. Bring milk to a boil and gradually stir in rice and water mixture. Stirring constantly, cook until thickened.

3. Add sugar and continue to cook until sugar is dissolved. Add 1 tsp orange juice and simmer for 5 minutes.

4. Pour into individual serving dishes and sprinkle with chopped nuts.

Turkish Pastries

(36 pastries)

INGREDIENTS

3 oz phylo sheets
1 cup cream cheese
1 egg lightly beaten

$\frac{1}{4}$ cup melted butter
1 tbsp chopped parsley

PREPARATION

1. Cut the phylo sheets (see p. 203) into 3-inch squares. Working with a few at a time, keep the rest covered with a damp towel.

2. Combine cheese, egg, and parsley. Put a spoonful of cheese mixture on each square and roll like small cigars; cover with a damp towel.

3. Place on a cookie sheet, coat lightly with melted butter. Bake in a preheated 350° oven for from 10 to 12 minutes or until lightly browned.

Greece

Lamb Baked in Packages

(4 servings)

INGREDIENTS

2 lb leg of lamb cut into 4
serving portions
4 1-inch cubes feta cheese
4 small carrots split lengthwise
8 small stalks celery with leaves

4 medium potatoes peeled,
halved, and parboiled
lemon juice
salt and pepper

PREPARATION

1. Place each serving of lamb on a square of heavy aluminum foil. On each piece of meat arrange a square of feta cheese, 1 carrot, 1 stalk celery, and 1 potato. Add a few drops of lemon juice to each and sprinkle with salt and pepper.

2. Make a tight foil package to seal in flavors. Arrange packages close together in a baking pan.

3. Bake in a preheated 350° oven for 2½ hours.

4. Serve in packages.

Lamb Stew

(6 servings)

INGREDIENTS

2 lb cubed leg of lamb
3 onions minced
4 tbsp butter
1 tbsp tomato paste

1 cup water
salt and pepper
2 sprigs parsley chopped

PREPARATION

1. Melt butter in large skillet and brown meat on both sides over high heat. Reduce heat to moderate, add onion, and brown lightly.

2. Add tomato paste mixed with water and salt and pepper to taste.

3. Cover tightly and cook over low heat for from 1½ to 2 hours or until meat is tender and sauce is thick. Sprinkle with chopped parsley.

Skewered Lamb

(6 servings)

INGREDIENTS

1 lb leg of lamb
1 cup olive oil
⅓ cup lemon juice
½ cup red wine
2 cloves garlic chopped
coarsely ground salt
dash of pepper

1 tsp oregano
1 bay leaf
4 tomatoes quartered
1 large onion
2 green peppers
8 mushrooms

PREPARATION

1. Cut the meat from leg of lamb into cubes about 1½ inches to a side. Place the lamb in a deep bowl and sprinkle it with olive oil, lemon juice, wine, garlic, salt and pepper, oregano, and bay leaf. Toss the ingredients together until thoroughly blended. Weight with a heavy plate and marinate in refrigerator overnight or for at least 6 hours.

2. Cut tomatoes in quarters. Cut onion in quarters and separate the layers. Seed peppers and cut into strips 1 inch wide; wipe the mushrooms with a damp paper towel and cut off tough ends of the stems.

3. Arrange meat cubes on skewers alternating with tomatoes, onions, green pepper, and mushrooms.

4. Cook over charcoal or under broiler until browned on all sides. Turn occasionally and baste with the marinade. Do not overcook. The meat should be about medium rare. Serve with Arab bread (p. 189) and yogurt sauce (below).

Yogurt Sauce

(1½ cups)

INGREDIENTS

1 cucumber peeled and seeded

1 cup plain yogurt

1 tbsp olive oil
3 walnuts chopped
3 cloves garlic mashed
2 tbsp vinegar or lemon juice

½ tsp salt
dash of pepper
dash of monosodium glutamate

PREPARATION

1. Grate cucumber and drain off liquid.
2. Combine with remaining ingredients and stir until completely combined. Season with salt and pepper to taste. Chill and serve with Arab bread (p. 189) and skewered lamb.

Stuffed Grape Leaves (1)

(30 rolls)

INGREDIENTS

1 cup olive oil
3 large onions chopped and
   lightly salted
¼ tsp pepper
1 cup rice washed and drained
1 tbsp chopped fresh dill or
   1 tsp dry dill

½ cup chopped parsley leaves
   and stems
5–6 green onions minced
2 lemons
2 cups water
½ lb jar grape leaves in brine
1 tsp salt

PREPARATION

1. Heat ½ cup olive oil and sauté rice and onions until onions are transparent. Add pepper and cook for 10 minutes, stirring occasionally. Add dill, parsley, green onions, juice of 1 lemon, and ½ cup of water. Cook for 10 minutes or until the liquid is absorbed. Correct seasoning with salt and pepper.

2. Rinse grape leaves, separate carefully, and spread them, shiny side down, on a flat surface. Put 1 tsp filling on each grape leaf near the base. Starting at the base, fold over the filling. Fold sides in then roll tightly toward the tip.

3. Arrange the rolls in layers in a kettle with parsley among the layers. Add remaining ½ cup olive oil, juice of the remaining lemon, and 1 cup water. Weight with a heavy plate and simmer for 25 minutes. Add ½ cup water and simmer for 25 minutes longer.

4. Cool and serve with additional lemon juice.

Stuffed Grape Leaves (2)

(approximately 70 rolls)

INGREDIENTS

1 cup olive oil

3 large onions chopped

1 tsp salt

¼ tsp pepper

1 cup rice washed and drained

1 lb ground beef or lamb

¼ cup chopped fresh parsley with stems

1 cup lemon juice

2½ cups beef bouillon

3 eggs lightly beaten

1 quart grape leaves in brine

½ tsp monosodium glutamate

PREPARATION

1. Heat ½ cup olive oil and in it sauté onions until transparent. Add pepper, meat, rice, and parsley. Cook for 10 minutes or until the meat is brown, stirring occasionally. Add ½ cup of lemon juice and ½ of the beef bouillon. Cover and simmer for 25 minutes or until the liquid is absorbed. Season with salt, pepper, and monosodium glutamate.

2. Rinse grape leaves, separate carefully, and place them shiny side down on a flat surface. Put 1 tsp filling prepared in preceding step on each grape leaf. Starting at base, fold leaf over filling; next fold sides over and roll tightly toward the tips.

3. Arrange the rolls in the bottom of large pot. Sprinkle with remaining ½ cup lemon juice, ½ cup olive oil, and beef bouillon. Place a heavy plate on the rolls to weight them. Cover pot and simmer for 35 minutes.

4. Remove stuffed leaves to cool; reserve liquid.

5. To beaten eggs very slowly add reserved liquid, stirring constantly. Cook this mixture over low heat, stirring occasionally, until it starts to thicken.

6. Cool the thickend sauce slightly. Pour over stuffed grape leaves and store in refrigerator until ready to serve.

Stewed Green Beans

(4-6 servings)

INGREDIENTS

1 lb green beans

1 small onion minced

¼ cup butter
1 clove garlic minced
1 tsp fresh mint leaves minced
1 tbsp parsley minced

1 tsp fennel seeds
½ cup tomato paste
¼ cup water
salt and pepper to taste

PREPARATION

1. Sauté onion in butter until golden.

2. Wash and trim beans. Cut beans into 2-inch lengths. Add to onion and, stirring constantly, sauté with a little salt until beans have turned bright green.

3. Add remaining ingredients and simmer for 30 minutes or until the beans are tender.

Flat Bread 1

(12 loaves)

INGREDIENTS

1 package (13¾ oz) hot-roll mix   12 6½-inch squares of foil
coarse crystal salt

PREPARATION

1. Prepare hot-roll mix according to package directions or prepare yeast-risen rolls by your favorite recipe. When dough has doubled in bulk, place it on a floured board and knead lightly. Divide into 12 equal pieces.

2. Pat each piece of dough into a ball; then using a rolling pin, roll each ball into a circle 6 inches in diameter and ¼ inch thick. Place each round on a square of aluminum foil and sprinkle lightly with salt. Let stand uncovered at room temperature for 1 hour.

3. Place rack at lowest position and preheat oven to 400°. Bake the bread on foil placed directly on oven rack for 5 to 6 minutes or until puffed and lightly browned.

4. Remove and serve at once with butter.

Flat Bread 2

This typical Arabic bread frequently serves as placemat, plate, spoon, and fork. It is a large, round, lightly leavened, flat loaf that dries out quickly because it contains no milk or shortening. A portion of dough is reserved each day to be used as a starter in making the next batch.

INGREDIENTS

2 envelopes active dry yeast	3 cups water
2½ cups lukewarm water	1 tbsp coarse crystal salt
2 tbsp sugar	olive oil
11½ cups sifted all-purpose flour	aluminum foil

PREPARATION

1. Soften 2 envelopes active dry yeast in 2½ cups lukewarm water, stir in 2 tbsp sugar and 2½ cups flour. Let stand overnight.

2. The following morning stir in 3 cups water, 1 tbsp salt, and about 9 cups flour, or enough to make a stiff dough. Turn out on a floured board or pastry sheet and knead until smooth.

3. Place in large oiled bowl and grease the top lightly with olive oil. Cover and let rise in a warm place until doubled in size, about 1½ hours.

4. Punch down and shape into a long thick roll. Set aside about one third of the roll for a starter for the next batch of bread.

5. Cut remaining roll into slices. Form each slice into a ball. Using a rolling pin, on a floured board roll each ball into a circle 6 inches in diameter and ¼ inch thick. Place each round on a 6-inch squares of aluminum foil. Let stand uncovered at room temperature for 1 hour.

6. Place oven rack at the lowest position and preheat oven to 400°. Sprinkle the loaves with salt and bake them 2 at a time.

7. Bake about 5 to 6 minutes, or until puffed and just golden. They should be crisp and slightly bubbly on top.

8. Next day, dissolve starter in 3 cups salted water and stir in enough flour to make a stiff dough. Let rise and follow recipe for shaping and baking.

Chicken and Lemon Soup with Kufta Meatballs

(6 servings)

BROTH

6 cups chicken stock	juice of 1½ lemons
⅓ cup white rice	1 tsp dehydrated parsley flakes
3 eggs	

KUFTA (28 tiny meatballs)

½ lb ground lamb
¼ lb ground beef
¼ cup dry bread crumbs
1 egg yolk
1 small onion minced

1 tsp salt
½ tsp pepper
¼ tsp allspice
2 tbsp chopped parsley
1 tbsp vegetable oil

PREPARATION

1. Combine all meatball ingredients except oil. Form into 28 balls the size of large marbles. In a skillet heat oil and add meatballs. Sauté over low heat until done. Drain well.

2. Bring chicken stock to boil in large saucepan. Add rice and meatballs. Simmer covered for 20 minutes. Add parsley.

3. Beat eggs with lemon juice and gradually stir in 1½ cups of the hot broth. Slowly add egg-lemon mixture to the broth; do not let the soup boil. Return to heat and simmer, stirring constantly, until egg is cooked—about 1 minute. Serve at once.

Fish-roe Dip

(4 or more hors d'oeuvre servings)

INGREDIENTS

3 tbsp red caviar or any
   available salted fish roe in
   oil
3 slices of white bread, trimmed,
   soaked in water, and drained

½ clove garlic mashed
2–3 tbsp fresh lemon juice
¾ cup olive oil
¼ tsp monosodium glutamate

PREPARATION

1. Using a large mortar, a bowl and wooden spoons, an electric beater, or a blender (low speed) thoroughly combine roe and lemon juice.

2. Add bread and garlic and continue to beat at medium speed. While beating, gradually add oil. Correct seasoning with more lemon juice if desired. Constantly beat until mixture is a moderately firm purée. If it is too thick or dry, thin with a few drops of water.

3. Pile on serving plate and surround with green-pepper sections, tomatoes, cucumber, lettuce leaves, and olives.

Pickled Squid

(6 servings)

INGREDIENTS

2 lb fresh squid
¾ cup vinegar
1 tsp pickle spices tied in a
   cheesecloth bag

2 tbsp olive oil
salt and pepper to taste

PREPARATION

1. Clean the fresh squid under cold running water. Remove fins and tentacles; peel off and discard the lacy outer membrane. Pat the squid dry with paper towels.

2. Heat olive oil in a skillet. Add squid, cover, and cook over low heat for 30 minutes, or until squid is tender. Drain.

3. Combine squid with the remaining ingredients.

4. Bring liquid to a boil and simmer for 5 minutes. Discard spice bag. Cover and refrigerate for 3 days or more. Serve cold.

Cheese Pastries

(24 pastries)

INGREDIENTS

1½ tbsp butter
1½ tbsp flour
¾ cup hot milk
½ egg yolk
1 egg

⅛ tsp pepper
⅓ lb feta cheese finely crumbled
1 lb (2 sticks) butter melted
2 phylo pastry sheets

Phylo pastry is available at all Middle Eastern groceries or bakeries. It is so difficult to prepare that even cooks in that region purchase it from professionals.

PREPARATION

1. In a saucepan melt 1½ tbsp butter. Add flour and cook, stirring, until well blended.

2. Remove from heat and add hot milk. Mix with a wire whisk until blended. Return to heat and cook, stirring with the whisk, until the sauce is smooth and thick.

3. Beat eggs and egg yolk with a little of the hot sauce. Stir into sauce and cook over low heat, whisking constantly for 2 minutes.

4. Remove from heat and stir in pepper and cheese.

5. Cut phylo pastry sheets into long strips 2 inches wide. Brush each strip with melted butter. Place one tbsp of the cheese mixture at one end and fold over and over again into a small triangle. With each fold, make sure that the bottom edge is parallel with the alternate edge.

6. Arrange the triangles on a baking sheet. Bake in a preheated 425° oven for from 10 to 15 minutes or until golden brown.

Nut Pastry

(4 servings)

INGREDIENTS

8 eggs separated	1 cup sweet butter melted
$\frac{1}{2}$ cup sugar	16 phylo pastry sheets
8 oz toasted almonds ground	1 tsp cinnamon
8 oz walnut meats ground	1 tsp almond extract
1 tsp baking powder	2 tbsp brandy

SYRUP

3 cups sugar	$\frac{1}{4}$ cup honey
$1\frac{1}{2}$ cups water	juice of $\frac{1}{2}$ lemon

PREPARATION

1. Beat egg yolks and $\frac{1}{2}$ cup sugar until mixture is very thick and pale in color. Beat at high speed for 2 minutes longer. Fold in almonds, walnuts, baking powder, cinnamon, almond extract, and cognac.

2. Beat egg whites until stiff but not dry. Carefully fold into the yolk-nut mixture. This is best done with both hands.

3. Line a 9 x 13 inch baking pan with 8 sheets of phylo pastry; butter each sheet. Turn egg-nut mixture into the pan and top with 8 more buttered phylo sheets. Make a few long slits in the pastry with a sharp knife and bake in a preheated 350° oven for about 50 minutes or until golden brown. Keep warm.

4. Remove from oven and cut into diamond-shaped serving pieces.

5. In a saucepan combine 3 cups sugar, $1\frac{1}{2}$ cups water, $\frac{1}{4}$ cup honey, and juice of $\frac{1}{2}$ lemon. Bring to a boil and simmer for 30 minutes. Cool. Pour cold syrup over the pastry.

Appendix

1. General Ingredients

The following general notes on ingredients used in oriental cooking are intended to be only a guide. Most of the foodstuffs called for in this book are available in large markets or oriental and Middle Eastern speciality shops. As is true of all fine cooking, oriental recipes are best made with the ingredients for which they are designed, but wherever substitutions produce comparable results, I have indicated them.

Azuki

Azuki are small red beans not unlike lentils in appearance. They are cooked with glutinous rice to make a special Japanese holiday food (see p. 122) or more often they are boiled till soft, mashed, and sweetened for use in a wide variety of sweet foods. For greater cooking convenience it is better to purchase this sweetened paste canned in oriental markets. It comes in two kinds: koshian, in which the skins of the beans have been completely mashed to form a smooth paste; tsuboan, in which the skins of the beans remain more or less intact.

Bamboo Shoots

This delicious, crunchy vegetable is ubiquitous in the Far East and is a seasonal favorite in the spring. Tender shoots are canned for later use. Canned bamboo shoots are usually available in oriental markets and in well stocked supermarkets. Large wedges packed in water are easiest to use. After opening, drain and store in fresh water in a covered container in the refrigerator. If you change the water daily bamboo shoots can be kept for approximately ten days.

Bean Curd

To make this smooth, white custard-like food, dried soy beans are soaked and mashed. The resultant watery pulp is strained through cloth to make a milky substance, which is then solidified by means of additions of magnesium chloride. Highly nutritious, bean curd contains in addition to vitamins A, B, and G, so high a percentage of protein that it is considered a good meat substitute. Oriental markets sell bean curd in blocks stored in clear water or refrigerated. Canned bean curd is less delicately flavored than the fresh product, but its texture makes it desirable for certain foods. Bean curd will last in the refrigerator for about ten days. Chinese markets sometimes sell it cut in small cubes.

When bean curd is cut into smaller rectangles, triangles, or cubes and deep-fat fried it is called aburaage in Japanese.

A variation of bean curd is made by boiling the soy bean milk, causing it to separate into an upper creamy layer and a sediment. Both products are then dried to form glazed, board-like substances which may be stored easily. After cooking, these apparently unappetizing boards become creamy and soft. The sediment is generally used in Chinese fish dishes and the creamy layer in soups.

Bird's Nests
Another of the exotic ingredients regarded very highly by Chinese gourmets is the nest of swift native to Malaya, Siam, Sumatra, and Borneo. This very special bird makes its home from a gelatinous material obtained from seaweed and from small fish that the swifts mix with saliva. Considered very nutritious, the nests are invariably served in soups at formal Chinese dinners. They are also used in sweet foods. The nests are dried and purified; and before being cooked, they must be soaked. They are available in most Chinese speciality shops in dry, porous, brittle cakes made from ground whole nests. The following is the procedure for making bird's nest soup. Place $\frac{1}{2}$ box bird's nests in a heavy pot with 4 cups of cold water. Simmer over a low heat for 1 hour. Set this aside as you heat shredded cooked chicken or pork in 6 cups of chicken stock. Add 2 tsp salt and $\frac{1}{2}$ tsp monosodium glutamate and the nests. Garnish with green onions if desired.

Bitter Melon
About the size of a cucumber, this melon, which is a kind of balsam pear, has a wrinkled green skin. Its inner layer of spongy pulp and seeds must be scooped out before cooking. After proper preparation, the melon has a cool, slightly bitter taste that one soon comes to appreciate. The presence of quinine accounts for the bitterness.

Burdock

Burdock root, called gobo in Japanese, is a pleasing addition to many variety vegetable dishes because of its mild, unusual flavor. A root, sometimes several feet long, it is covered with a thin skin that must be scraped off. But since burdock discolors quickly, it must be kept in water until time to add it to the food being prepared. In addition, since it is slightly astringent, burdock is often soaked in acidulated water for a few minutes prior to use. It is available canned and fresh, but both versions require care to prevent discoloring. If refrigerated, burdock will keep for about 2 weeks, but it must not be scraped or cut before storing.

Chard

This inexpensive all-year vegetable is called shirona or shakushina in Japanese and bok choy in Chinese. With something of the appearance of Swiss chard, the oriental vegetable has young milky-white stalks, loose green leaves at the ends, and a yellow flower in the center. Winter crops are considered choice.

Chinese (Celery) Cabbage

The long whitish head of Chinese celery cabbage—hakusai in Japanese and sieu choy or wong nga fok in Chinese—has light green, crinkly end leaves. Although used in many casseroles and braised dishes, it is most popular in pickles, which are commercially available bottled or bagged.

Coconut

The fruit of the coconut palm is familiar all over the world in dried or canned forms, but neither of these can equal fresh coconut for flavor and texture. The milk with which the seed is filled is an important ingredient in many dishes, especially those of the Pacific region and Southeast Asia. When purchasing fresh coconut, always shake the fruit to make certain that it contains plenty of milk. Never buy a cracked coconut. An average coconut—about $1\frac{1}{2}$ pounds—will yield from 3 to 4 cups of chopped or grated coconut meat.

At one end of the coconut are eyelike spots. To drain the milk puncture 2 or 3 or these spots with an icepick or screw driver. To crack the shell, tap it with the back of a clever all around the periphery at a point about one-third the way from the punctured end. You will be able to pry the top off easily by inserting a screw driver into the thin crack that will develop at this place. Special Chinese graters for coconut are available, but diced coconut meat may be reduced to the desired consistency more conveniently in an electric blender.

"Coconut milk" in recipes in this book refers either to the natural milk or to an essence prepared in the following way. Pour $\frac{1}{2}$ cup boiling water over 3 or 4 cups grated coconut. Press the coconut down into the liquid with a wooden spoon. Allow this to stand for about 20 minutes and then strain through a double layer of cheesecloth. Squeeze well to extract all the liquid. This should produce about 1 cup of coconut milk. If tightly covered the milk will keep about 5 days in the refrigerator.

Coconut cream may be made in two ways. Allow natural coconut milk to stand at room temperature for 1 hour or more until it separates. The cream may then be skimmed from the top. If natural coconut milk is unavailable, combine 2 cups milk, 2 cups heavy cream, 1 cup water, 1 tsp salt, and $1\frac{1}{3}$ cups grated coconut in a saucepan. Bring this to a boil, reduce heat, and simmer for 10 minutes. Strain through a double layer of cheesecloth, squeezing well to extract all the cream.

Daikon

Daikon, a long white radish, ranges in length from 6 inches to several feet. Most plentiful and delicious in winter, it is crisp, tender, and mild.

Daikon, which may be kept refrigerated for up to 2 weeks, occurs in relishes, stews, and salads and as a condiment in Japan, China, and Korea.

Daikon oroshi is a grated daikon garnish for tempura and casserole dishes. Momiji oroshi is made from daikon into which dried, seeded red peppers are inserted. The daikon is later grated and drained; the pepper gives it a reddish tint like that of maple leaves, or momiji.

Takuan is a Japanese pickle made from daikon tinted yellow. It may be purchased in bottles or open barrels in Japanese markets or in refrigerated plastic bags.

Dried Mushrooms   See Shiitake.

Feta Cheese

This white cheese made from sheep or goat milk is available in Middle Eastern grocery stores.

Fu

This very light cake made from wheat gluten is available in white or pastel colors. It is often used in soups.

Ghee
Ghee is merely clarified butter. Many Indian cooks heat ghee in a ladle and add the spices to this before including them in the dish they are preparing.

Gingko Nuts
The tough-shelled nuts of the gingko tree are available fresh and canned in oriental speciality shops. The delightful, slightly bitter, flavor of the flesh of the nut is a delicious addition to many dishes. Like the chestnut, however, they require labor for they have a number of protective coverings that must be removed. First the soft outer covering must be washed off. Then the hard, white shell must be cracked and removed. Finally a filmy inner skin must be peeled away. Once opened, gingko nuts will keep tightly covered in the refrigerator for several weeks.

Hoisin Sauce
This piquant, sweet-spicy Chinese sauce has an overtone of plum flavor though it is made from soy beans, garlic, salt, ginger, and chili. It may be used as a table condiment; in making marinades for Peking duck, shell fish, and other dishes; or on roast or barbecued pork. Generally sold in one-pound cans, hoisin sauce may be stored for several months refrigerated in a tightly covered container.

Japanese Pork Cutlet (Tonkatsu) Sauce
Made from apples and soy sauce, this thick, spicy sauce is sold ready prepared in Japanese markets. It is the favorite for flavoring and dipping different kinds of foods but especially the fried pork cutlet (tonkatsu) beloved of the Japanese working people.

Jellyfish
After being preserved in salt and alum, jellyfish are dried in thin or thick sheets. Before they can be used, the thin sheets must be soaked in cold water for three days; the thicker sheets take four days to soften. The soaked jellyfish must then be rinsed. Only the amount needed for a given recipe is shredded, covered with hot water, soaked, and drained again. The remainder of the sheet will keep for two weeks if the water in which it is stored is changed daily. The Chinese consider jellyfish a great delicacy.

Kamaboko Fish Loaf

Kamaboko is made by pounding the flesh of white fish, seasoning the resulting pulp, adding a thickening agent—for instance arrowroot starch—shaping it into small loaves, and steaming it. The result is a white, fish-flavored substance slightly firmer than frankfurter sausages. It is eaten sliced and cold with soy sauce or included in several cooked foods. Kamaboko, which is sold in most Japanese food stores, requires refrigeration.

Kampyo

The flesh of the bottle gourd that is the fruit of a vine called the moonflower is cut into strips and dried as a foodstuff called kampyo. After the strips have been softened in water, they are used as garnishes, in tying such foods as stuffed cabbage leaves, and even to plug the holes in abalone shells used as containers for foods. See p. 105 for the way kampyo is prepared for use in sushi.

Katsuobushi

This dried flesh of the bonito is traditionally sold in moderately large pieces and shaved as needed for the preparation of stocks for a number of dishes. But today it is available already shaved and packaged in bags. Katsuobushi will keep indefinitely.

Kikurage

Although most unimpressive in the dried state in which it is usually sold, this cultivated fungus is nutritious and delicious when softened in water for a few minutes. It then expands into a beautiful, transluscent form not unlike the shape of a human ear. Though gelatinous in appearance, it retains a crunchy texture. The Chinese call kikurage wun yec and use it in toss-fried, combination vegetable dishes.

Konnyaku

This firm, jelly-like substance is made by cooking a mixture of milk of lime and the pulp of the tuber of a plant called devil's tongue. It is sold in blocks and in threadlike lengths about the size of vermicelli called shirataki. It is available canned in Japanese markets and will keep for a moderately long time under refrigeration.

Lotus Root

The root of the lotus plant is dug from the mud, washed, peeled, and sliced for use in many foods, especially vinegared dishes (see p. 107).

In the West it is generally available canned in oriental markets. Seeds from the dried pods of lotus blossoms are used in some Chinese dishes.

Matsutake
Possibly one of the most delicious of all mushrooms, the matsutake in Japan grows only at the roots of red pines. Since it cannot be artificially cultivated, its season lasts for only a few weeks in the autumn, and its prices are high. Traditionally it is either grilled with a light marinade of soy sauce and sweet sake or steamed with shrimp, chicken, gingko nuts, and chestnuts in a delicious dish called dobin mushi (p. 103). It is also sometimes cooked with rice, chicken, and vegetables for a special seasonal treat. Canned matsutake are sold in Japanese markets, and in the United States limited amounts of fresh ones go on sale in November, the matsutake season in Seattle, Washington.

Mirin See Sake.

Miso
Not strictly a sauce, this bean paste is made by crushing boiled soy beans and, after adding wheat or rice for fermentation, allowing the mixture to stand for about two months. It is often used in making dressings for vegetables. It is also an important ingredient in marinades for fish, vegetables, or meat; but its most famous role is that of flavoring for the popular Japanese soup called miso-shiru. Available in all Japanese markets, miso will keep for as long as a year at room temperature. It comes in two basic types: mild white or shiro-miso and stronger red or aka-miso.

Mustard Greens
The strongly flavored, deep apple-green leaves of the mustard plant—karashina in Japanese and gai choy in Chinese—are sometimes ten or twelve inches long. When cooked properly, mustard greens turn a magnificent jade green color.

Nameko
These small mushrooms coated with a slippery amber substance have a tantalizing woody flavor. They are used most widely in soup. Canned nameko are on sale in most Japanese markets.

Noodles
Made from wheat, rice, or buckwheat, noodles are an important part of the oriental diet, especially in Japan, where they are a favorite lunch or

snack dish. Representative Japanese noodles, available in most oriental markets, include udon, a thick wheat-flour noodle; somen, finer wheat noodles usually served cold and often colored delicate pastel colors; hiyamugi, thin, white noodles also served cold; and soba, buckwheat-flour noodles popularly served in hot soup with a number of different kinds of garnishes.

The general Chinese word for noodles—mein—covers many sizes and shapes that can be served in several ways. The popular American dish called chow mein is made of Chinese noodles deep-fat fried and covered in a sauce of braised vegetables and meats. The fad for instant foods has invaded the traditional field of noodle dishes, and many kinds are sold in large markets and specialty stores. They are easy to cook but decidedly inferior to noodles prepared in the proper ways.

Won ton is a noodle-like pastry generally sold in 3-inch squares. These are often filled with meat or other farce ingredients and simmered in soups, but they may be deep-fat fried and served with savory sauces or mustard.

Harusame are fine, transparent noodles made of bean gelatin. They must be softened in cold water before using.

Oyster Sauce

This strong, salty sauce, which is available in most oriental markets, is made from oysters, though the taste of the shellfish is all but totally obscured in the cooking process. It is used as a seasoning or a condiment.

Peppers

These widely used members of the capiscum family range in color from red to green and in taste from mild to fiery. Cayenne is a ground seasoning made from very hot red peppers. In the Orient, more than one variety of peppers are combined to make powders for adding piquance to many different dishes. One of the most representative of these combination peppers is the Japanese shichimi-togarashi (seven-flavored pepper) which includes cayenne, sesame seed, sansho (a distinctive Japanese pepper), hemp seed, poppy seed, orange peel, and rape seed. Available in mild, medium, and strong, shichimi-togarashi is found most often in noodle and casserole dishes.

A Japanese green chili pepper called shishito is mild and sweet in flavor. Standard green bell peppers may be substituted for it.

The chili powder, popular in Mexican foods, is said to have resulted from the experimentation of a Texan attempting to approximate curry powders he had eaten in India.

Paprika, a common seasoning and garnish for vegetables, meats, salad, soups, and other foods, is a bright red powdered pepper with a very mild flavor.

Phylo Pastry

This thin pastry is considered so difficult to make that even Middle-Eastern housewives purchase it prepared instead of making it themselves. It is usually stocked by stores specializing in Middle Eastern foods.

Plum Sauce

Roast duck, roast or barbecued pork, beef, and other meats are dipped in this thick, dark brown, piquant sauce for flavor accent. Plums, apricots, chili, vinegar, and sugar are used in its preparation. Plum sauce is sold in both cans and bottles in most oriental food stores, and it can be stored refrigerated for several months. It is wise, however, to transfer the plum sauce from the can to a nonmetal, covered container before putting it in the refrigerator.

Rice

Rice, one of the most important of all the cereals and a staple food in many lands, is roughly categorized into short-grain, medium-grain, and long-grain types. Medium-grain rice is preferred for Japanese cooking because of its moisture-retaining properties that make it palatable even when cold. Long-grain rice, which requires more water and more time to cook, is widely used with Chinese food. A special glutinous rice is cooked and pounded into a New Year treat called mochi, which is about the texture of taffy when warm but which hardens quickly and must be reheated before being eaten. Flour made from glutinous rice is used in making cakes and pastries and thin brittle noodles.

In general, rice for oriental dinners is prepared in roughly the same way that is used wherever the grain is eaten, but the following few hints will guarantee success in producing the glossy, moist quality prized by Japanese gourmets. About one hour before cooking time, wash the rice several times until the water runs completely clear. Drain it in a colander. To cook oriental, medium-grain rice use 5 cups rice to 6 cups water. Rice grown in the West in dry fields instead of in paddies requires more water: 7 to 9 cups water to 5 of rice. Combine the rice and water in a heavy pot with a closely fitting lid. Over a high heat, bring the water to a boil. Lower the heat and cook until all the moisture has been absorbed. Remove the pot from the heat and allow the rice to stand covered for 10 minutes before serving.

Modern electric rice cookers with calibrations indicating the correct amounts of water to use for given quantities of rice make rice cooking foolproof and easy. Be sure that you follow the directions given by the maker of the cooker.

Rice Vinegar
When preparing Japanese foods that call for vinegar, always use rice vinegar, which is milder than most Western vinegars.

Sake
The famous Japanese rice wine is widely sold in liquor stores in the West. It comes in several grades and in slightly sweet or dry varieties. Although dry sherry is often suggested as a substitute, the results are not as good as they are when sake is used. Mirin is a very sweet rice wine used as a seasoning and in a traditional Japanese New Year ceremonial drink call otoso. Once again, optimum results cannot be obtained by using sweet sherry in place of mirin, though it may be substituted if the true sweet wine is unavailable.

Seaweeds
All of the edible sea plants are rich sources of minerals, iodine, and vitamin C. In addition they are easily digested.

1. Kelp, or dashi kombu in Japanese. Sold in oriental markets in tough, blackish sheets that keep indefinitely, kelp is the basis of the delicately flavored broth used in many Japanese soups and braised foods.

2. Wakame. These long, curly strands of dried seaweed must be soaked, washed, and stripped from the central stem, which is tough. They may be used in salads and soups. Most oriental markets stock wakame.

3. Nori or laver. This is finer seaweed pressed into paper-thin sheets and dried on smooth surfaces. A rich, blackish green color, it becomes crisp and turns slightly purple when toasted. It is delicious dipped in soy sauce and eaten with freshly steamed rice or as a garnish for other food.

Shark's Fin
Another Chinese delicacy, shark's fins require considerable preparation because they come dried, either with or without the tough skin of the shark.

To prepare skinless fins follow this procedure. Soak ½ lb of fins in warm water for 30 minutes. Add 1 tsp bicarbonate of soda and simmer over a low heat for 2 hours. By this time, the fins will be soft and fragile. Remove the fins from the broth in which they were simmered and soak in warm water until ready to use.

To prepare the fins with the tough skin, follow this procedure. Boil 1 lb of fins in water for 1 hour. Remove the fins and wash them carefully to remove sand. Remove flesh or bone that may be clinging to the fins. Return to the pot, cover with fresh water, add 1 tsp of bicarbonate of soda, and simmer for 2 hours. Once again remove and store in clear water until ready to use. They may be refrigerated in this water.

Perhaps the most famous of all shark's fin dishes is a soup made in the following way. To 8 cups of chicken or meat stock add 1 tsp salt and ½ tsp monosodium glutamate. Add softened shark's fins (see above) and heat for 10 minutes. This soup may be made more elaborate by the addition of shredded, cooked chicken breast meat, celery, or Chinese cabbage. Though not as well known in the West, very delicious dishes are made from shark's fins with meats or chicken. These foods are a rich red color because they always incorporate soy sauce.

Shiitake (Dried Mushrooms)
Larger, more aromatic, and more flavorful than champignons, shiitake mushrooms are sold fresh in the Orient, though in other parts of the world they are usually available in dried form only. They add very special flavor to braised foods, soups, and other dishes. Dried shiitake must be softened in lukewarm water for about twenty minutes before using. In Japan these brown mushrooms are artificially cultivated in vast quantities, harvests taking place both in spring and fall.

Shirataki   See Konnyaku.

Snow Peas
Not exclusively oriental, these tiny pea pods are known in the West as sugar peas or under the French name mange tout. In oriental foods they are usually a garnish or an addition to stir-fried vegetable combi-

nations. Before cooking them, one must break off the tough tips and remove the stringy fiber running down the side of the pod. Though never expensive, they are cheapest in the months between May and September. They are usually available in both fresh and frozen forms.

Soy Sauce

This pungent, salty, brown sauce is made by a process of fermentation from wheat, yeast, salt, and soy beans, which are rich in proteins, vitamins A, B, and G, C, calcium, phosphorous, and iron. Though its origins are clouded in antiquity, soy sauce has been a necessity in Chinese and Japanese homes for many centuries. The first written mention of it seems to have been made in about 200 B.C., and numerous other references occur throughout oriental literature. It became an article of general commercial manufacture in 1688. Till that time it had been produced either in the home or as a village industry. For dishes in the oriental cuisines, soy sauces from China and Japan are the best.

Japanese soy sauce, or shoyu, is less salty and slightly sweeter than its Chinese counterpart because a larger amount of toasted wheat is used in its production. Its sharp flavor and exciting aroma have recently made it a popular seasoning all over the world. Several varieties, ranging in size from small containers to one-half or one-gallon bottles, are available. Some brands are slightly lighter in color than others, but all are brown.

Chinese soy sauce, or ch'iang-yu, ranges in color from light brown to a dark reddish brown and in density from thick to thin depending on grade and type.

Water Chestnuts

Certain varieties of this aquatic group of plants have edible seeds, but this is not true of the kind used in Chinese cooking. Called kuwai by the Japanese and mash tuy by the Chinese, the water chestnut found in braised and fried Chinese dishes is actually a hard tuber, the tough brown skin of which must be peeled off. But this crisp, slightly sweet delicacy is sold peeled and either sliced or whole in canned form. After being opened, canned water chestnuts must be drained, submerged in fresh water, and stored in the refrigerator, where they will keep for about a month if the water is changed daily.

2. Spices and Herbs

Allspice
Allspice is not a combination but a single spice made from the berry of the Pimenta officinalis plant, which grows abundantly in the West Indies. The English name derives from the fact that the spice seems to combine the tastes and fragrances of cinnamon, cloves and nutmeg. Interestingly enough, the Spanish named it pimento or pepper because the dried berry looks like an oversized peppercorn. The flavor of allspice is especially prized in making pies, cakes, cookies, and fruit compotes.

Bay Leaf
Bay leaves used in cooking grow on an evergreen shrub or tree called the laurel. The laurel family includes several other plants often employed as foods and flavorings: cinnamon, sassafras, avocado, camphor, and green heart. A native of southern Europe, laurel is widely grown in the United States. In ancient Greece, physicians held the laruel in high esteem as a promoter of good health. So great was their respect for it that they believed it protected them from poison and sorcery. When someone was gravely ill, a branch of laurel was hung at the door of his house to ward off death and evil spirits. The laurel crown was often used a symbol of victory.

The flavor of the bay or laurel leaf lends interest to meats, fish, poultry, stews, pickles, and soups; but it must not be used in great quantities for it can overpower other flavors. Generally one medium leaf is sufficient to season five or six servings.

Beefsteak Plant (Shiso)
Though not generally available in the West, the red and green leaves of this plant, widely used only in Japan and Vietnam, have an arresting flavor that does not, however, recall beefsteak in any way. In all probability the English name pertains to the red color of the leaves. Japanese use it in flavoring pickled ginger and pickled plums. The seeds are used to flavor sushi. In addition, the leaves are employed in a number of home remedies. The plant may be easily grown from seeds available in Japanese markets.

Caraway

It is generally believed that caraway originally came from Asia Minor many thousands of years ago. Caraway seeds have been found among debris left by primitive lake-dwelling people who lived 5,000 years ago. The plant belongs to the parsley family, and the seeds, familiar to Westerners mostly because of the aroma and taste they impart to rye bread, is a popular seasoning among peoples in all parts of the world. Today the Dutch grow large crops of caraway on the heavy clay land they have reclaimed from the North Sea. The heads of seed must be harvested during the wet night hours because they shatter easily when dried by the sun.

Cardamon

Cardamon, a member of the ginger family, is second in cost only to saffron among the spices of the world. Native to India and Southeast Asia, it thrives in warm, moist tropics where it is generally ripe throughout the year. The pods are snipped from the plants when about three-quarters ripe. Each straw-colored pod is about the size of a cranberry and contains from seventeen to twenty tiny, black, aromatic seeds. The pods themselves are discarded. The ancient Greeks and Romans used cardamon not only in foods, but also in medicines and perfumes. Its oil is still employed as an antiseptic and in the manufacture of scents. It is also used in making purgatives.

Cardamon is one of the principle ingredients in curry; and as might be expected in the light of this fact, it is most popular in India. Though its aroma is powerful, its taste is milder than might be thought.

Cinnamon

Two kinds of this famous spice share places of honor on the seasoning shelves of kitchens all over the world: Cinnamomum cassia and Cinnamomum zeylanicum.

Cinnamomum Cassis has an especially venerable history in China, where it was described in a work of the third century A.D. Its fame is even older, however, for the ancient Chinese regarded it as the tree of life growing in the garden of paradise believed to have been located at the headwaters of the Yellow River. Anyone who entered paradise and ate the fruit of this tree was thought to win immortality and eternal bliss. As a result of its wonderful attributes, Cinnamomum Cassia is used medicinally as a restorative and carminative. Even in eighteenth-century Europe, cinnamon waters were thought to cure gastritis. But in spite of its great reputation, the bark of this tree is coarse and woody and produces a less delicately flavored spice than Cinnamomum zeylanicum.

Cinnamomum zeylanicum, or Ceylonese cinnamon, is buff colored. It is popular in many parts of the world. The growing methods and sources of this spice have not altered in 3,000 years: Indonesia and South Vietnam still produce most of the world's supply. The trees themselves are moderate-sized evergreens. The bark, the part used in making spices and medicines, is harvested during the rainy seasons when moisture in the atmosphere makes it easy to handle. After it has been stripped from the trees, the bark is rolled into slender quills called cinnamon sticks.

In either stick or ground form, cinnamon adds tantalizing fragrance, pungency, slight sweetness, and astringency to all kinds of foods. The Greeks use it in beef stews, people in northern India employ it in curries, and the Mexicans are fond of putting it in chocolate. In Europe and the United States it is a major flavoring in many spicy desserts and baked foods.

Coriander
This aromatic herb of the parsley family was known to the Egyptians 3,000 years ago. Fresh coriander, sometimes called Chinese parsley, is more pungent in flavor than ordinary parsley. It is sold in bunches in oriental markets and will keep for about a week in the refrigerator if wrapped with paper towels or stored in plastic bags. Do not wash the leaves or remove the roots until you intend to use the coriander. Coriander seed, whole or ground, is a seasoning widely used in the Orient and many other parts of the world.

Cumin
Another of the essential ingredients in all curries, cumin was known to the ancient Egyptians and Jews. Though both are members of the parsley family, cumin and caraway have distinctly different flavors. Ground or whole cumin is used in flavoring meats, pickles, cheeses, sausages, soups, and stews.

Dill
Like caraway, dill is a member of the parsley family, and as is true of most other members of the group, it is best used fresh and whole,

though dried dill seeds and leaves are sometimes more readily available. Dill adds great interest to sour-cream sauces, green beans, cabbage, cucumbers, other vegetables, potato salad, or maccaroni and cheese. Fresh leaves are an excellent garnish for fish.

Fenugreek
The seeds of this annual Asiatic plant are used in curries and other foods. Fenugreek is usually available in ground form in markets with well-stocked spice departments.

Garam Masala
This mixture of spices is sprinkled on prepared foods in some parts of the Eastern world as a seasoning much as Westerners use salt and pepper. Although it is not always commercially available, it may be easily prepared by grinding together in a pepper mill the following: 2 tbsp black peppercorns, 2 tbsp coriander seeds, 5 tbsp caraway seeds, 1 tsp cardamon seeds, and about 1 or 2 tsp each of ground cinnamon and cloves.

Ginger
Ginger, among the first of the truly oriental spices to reach Alexandria and, from there, Greece and Rome, is mentioned by Dioscorides and Pliny. This would suggest that it must have been known in the West before the first century A.D. Furthermore, ginger appears often in a book or recipes by Apisius published during the heyday of Roman luxury. In addition to India, south China, and Japan, the British West Indies, Hawaii, and Puerto Rico are major producers of ginger.

The spice is made from the root of a lilylike plant. When the ginger is about one year old, the roots are dug, washed, and dried in the sun. Under a brown scaly skin is the rich, ivory-colored, slightly fibrous root, which may be sliced, ground, or treated in other ways.

Dried and ground ginger are available in most stores, but for Japanese and Chinese dishes, syrups, and pickling marinades whole fresh ginger is preferred. It is widely available and will keep for weeks unwrapped and refrigerated. Crystalized and syrup-packed gingers are confections; they are only rarely used as spices. Similarly, red pickled ginger, called beni-shoga in Japanese and soon geung in Chinese, is a condiment. An interesting quick pickle can be made by marinating delicate fiberless young ginger roots in a mixture of rice vinegar and sugar for a few hours. These pickles are a subtle addition to a number of meat and fish dishes. In addition to its many seasoning qualities, ginger will remove fishiness from seafoods without destroying their delicate sweetness.

Lemon Grass

Aromatic lemon or citronella grass is widely used in Indonesian and Southeast Asian cooking. It is available fresh in Hawaii and Puerto Rico though not on the mainland of the United States. Some nurseries will ship clipped roots in limited quantities to people who are interested in raising their own lemon grass. It multiplies rapidly, and from three to six roots will keep the average family more than adequately stocked in the spice. It may be grown outdoors in warm climates, but does not tolerate severe cold. For seasoning, slice the lower part of the stem below the blade crosswise as you would a scallion. Add it to soups and sauces for a lemon flavor. Lemon rind is sometimes substituted for this grass.

Matrimony Vine

Called kuko in Japanese and grow gay in Chinese, the matrimony vine is a member of the nightshade family. It has sharp thorns and leaves about one inch long. Because of the former, the leaves must be removed from the plant with great care. They are then added to soups and certain kinds of tea. The vine is a perennial. Preparations made from it are sometimes used as antiseptics and, carminatives. In the Middle Ages, cordials were made from the vine; and today the Japanese prepare a drink from the seeds steeped in sake with lemon peel, coriander seeds, nutmeg, cloves, cinnamon, and angelica root. It is available in oriental markets in fresh or dried leaves and seed or mixed with tea.

Monosodium Glutamate

In 1908, Dr. Kikunae Ikeda discovered that the secret of the delicious flavor imparted to Japanese soups by the use of a kind of kelp called kombu was the presence of an amino acid called glutamic acid. This important substance is refined from the kelp for kitchen use as a product called monosodium glutamate. In 1921, a Chinese scientist named Pool-Nien Wu, who lived in Shanghai, developed a process for extracting this same monosodium glutamate from wheat protein. Later his product was marketed throughout southern Asia and the Philippines in large amounts yearly. Other natural sources of the material include corn, soy-bean protein, and desugared beet molasses. The United

States manufacture billions of pounds of it each year. The recent discovery of a way to synthesize monosodium glutamate instead of extracting it from natural materials should greatly reduce its price.

All of the amino acids are of the greatest importance to the diet since they are components of protein. Glutamic acid, however, is sometimes called the parental amino because its functions in developing protein are extremely vital. In meat, fish, and vegetables the ordinary person takes in from one-half to two-thirds of an ounce of glutamic acid daily. In the body, monosodium glutamate taken as a flavor enhancer breaks down into glutamic acid and sodium, both of which the body requires. Monosodium glutamate is sold under several brand names.

Mustard

Man has been acquainted with the virtues of the seeds and oil of this family of plants since prehistoric times, and the Chinese used it many thousands of years ago. There are two basic mustard seed types: Brassica alba, which is either white or yellow, and Brassica junces, which is brown. Generally, mustard is sold in seed, powder, or the familiar prepared form. The hot mustard served in Chinese restaurants consists of brown oriental mustard mixed to a paste with water.

In addition to its value as a piquant addition to countless oriental and occidental foods, mustard has many medicinal uses. Mustard oil is good for the skin because it contains ergosterol. Rubbed into the skin and exposed to sunlight, mustard oil converts into vitamin D. Mustard oil is the basis of many unguents and of the familiar counterirritant mustard plaster.

Saffron

It is no wonder that saffron is the costliest of spices since to make one pound of the dried powder, the pollen must be removed from the stamens of 75,000 blossoms of a purple crocus called Crocus stivus. Saffron has been treasured from remotest times as a spice and coloring for foods, cosmetics, dyes, and medicines. Saffron may have originated in Israel, at any rate it is mentioned in the Song of Solomon as one of the chief spices, together with spikenard, calamus, cinnamon, frankincense, myrrh, and aloes. The taste of saffron, though pleasing when the spice is used moderately, becomes medicinal if too lavishly applied. A very small quantity—one-eighth of a teaspoon—will flavor and color a large pot of rice or curry.

Sansho Pepper

Sansho pepper is available ground in markets, but to obtain it fresh, it is necessary to grow the small thorny tree that produces it in one's garden. In Japan, cysts found on the leaves of the sansho tree are mixed with bean paste and vinegar to make a dressing. But the true fruit, which is ground and used as a condiment to reduce oiliness in foods and to cut the strong odors of certain fish, is a red, bony kernel enclosing a blackish-red, highly aromatic seed.

Sesame

Another of the most venerable seasonings and a source of rich, highly flavored oil, sesame has long been known and used in China and Japan. It is mentioned in the Old Testament. The white variety—shira goma in Japanese and chih mah in Chinese— is more common in the West; and black sesame—kuro goma or hak chih mah—is generally found only in oriental markets. Toasted or parched sesame seeds of either variety impart a welcome, delicate almondlike flavor to any dish in which chopped nutmeats might be used. They may be sprinkled untoasted on any dish that will brown lightly during cooking. Amber-colored sesame oil must be used more sparingly since its flavor is rich and pervasive. A few drops of it will liven soups or other bland foods. Sesame oil— goma abura in Japanese and gee mah you in Chinese—is sold canned or bottled in all oriental markets.

Star Anise

Though the seed of an entirely different plant, slightly bitter star anise tastes very much like true anise. The star anise shrub is an evergreen related to the magnolia and grown to heights of about ten feet. Its fruit is shaped like eight-pointed star, each point of which is a pod containing an aromatic oil that flavors the ingredients with which the pods are cooked. Chinese cooks regard star anise highly and use it to flavor meats. In addition, it is used as a stomach medicine and a carminative. A native of Southeast Asia and cultivated in China, star anise is not readily available in the United States, though some Chinese markets in larger cities stock it.

The Chinese use this spice in a potent, cocoa-colored combination together with cloves, fennel, cinnamon, and anise. This seasoning is unusual and powerful; it must be used with caution.

Tamarind

Tamarind is actually a tropical fruit consisting of a pod containing seeds in a juicy, spicy, sour pulp. The tree, which is an evergreen related to the legumes, is grown for its fragrant, red-streaked yellow flowers and its hard, heavy, yellowish woods. Tamarind is used as a seasoning in Malaysia and Indonesia. If it is unavailable, sour plums or apricots may be substituted for it. Indian, Latin American, and certain gourmet food stores sometimes handle dried tamarind pulp.

Turmeric

Another ancient oriental spice, turmeric is the root of a plant of the ginger family. Long a popular flavoring, it has also served as a dye, a ceremonial coloring, and an amulet. Today it is raised throughout Asia and in the Caribbean, or anywhere that ginger thrives. Because of its brilliant gold color, turmeric has often been associated with saffron. In fact in the Middle Ages it was called Indian saffron, or Crocus indicus. Many prepared mustards contain ground turmeric. In using it in cooking, always start with a small amount then taste to determine whether more is needed. The Japanese use turmeric to flavor the popular pickled daikon radish takuan. Medicinally the spice is thought to relive skin diseases, heal bruises, cure leech bits, and act as a carminative.

3. Sources for Oriental Foods

ALABAMA

International Gourmet
2308 Memorial Parkway S.W.,
Huntsville 35801

Toni's Oriental Food
Rt. 2, Box 259, Daleville 36322

ALASKA

Oriental Gardens
Klatt Box 10003, Anchorage 99502

ARIZONA

Oriental Food Center
3920 Grand Ave., Phoenix 85019

CALIFORNIA

SAN FRANCISCO, SACRAMENTO,
STOCKTON, MONTEREY AREAS

A-1 Fish Market
517 8th St., Oakland 94607

Albertson Market #717
3925 Alemany Blvd.,
San Francisco 94132

Alpha Beta Market #502
278 Bayfair Terrace,
San Leandro 94578

Alpha Beta Market #508
423 Santa Cruz Ave., Los Gatos 95030

American Fish Market
1836 Buchanan St.,
San Francisco 94115

Asahi Grocery
105 W. 8th St., Santa Rosa 95401

Bazaar
1717 N. 1st St., San Jose 95112

Castro City Grocery
40 S. Rengstorff Ave.,
Mountain View 94040

Chong Kee Jan Co.
35 Brenham Place,
San Francisco 94108

The Co-op Store
1581 University Ave.,
Berkeley 94703

Dobashi Co.
240 E. Jackson St., San Jose 95112

Econ Market
201 N. Bayshore Blvd.,
San Mateo 94401

Farmers Market No. 16
700 Onstott Rd., Yuba City 95991

Food Center Market
1912 Fruitridge, Sacramento 95822

Jacks Food Center
519 E. Charter Way, Stockton 95206

Japan Food Corp.
900 Marin St., San Francisco 94124

Lick Super Market
350 7th Ave., San Francisco 94118

Lincoln Market
2070 Lincoln Ave., Alameda 94501

Mayfair Market #123
Webster & Geary St.,
San Francisco 94115

Mayfair Market #149
340 3rd St., San Rafael 94901

Mission Market
20848 Mission Blvd., Hayward 94541

Naks Oriental Market
1151 Chestnut St., Menlo Park 94025

Nob Hill General Store
450 Westwood Shopping Center,
Gilroy 95020

Nori's
1215 W. Texas St., Fairfield 94533

Okazaki Co.
20 S. Main St., Lodi 95240

Pajaro Valley Fish Market
114 Union St., Watsonville 95076

Park & Shop Market
1200 Irving St., San Francisco 94122

Q. F. I.
64 Serramonte Blvd., Daly City 94015
(Serramonte Shopping Center)

Safeway Store #465
570 Munras Ave., Monterey 93940

Safeway Store #488
1720 Fremont Blvd., Seaside 93955

Safeway Store #509
32nd & Clement St.,
San Francisco 94118

Safeway Store #592
7th & Cabrillo St.,
San Francisco 94121

Safeway Store #613
2020 Shattuck St., Berkeley 94704

Safeway Store #664
27300 Hesperian Blvd.,
Hayward 94545

Safeway Store #711
15 Marina Blvd., San Francisco 94123

Safeway Store #749
Rio Highway #1, Carmel 93921

Safeway Store #761
1212 Forest Ave., Pacific Grove 93950

Safeway Store #768
20629 Redwood Rd.,
Castro Valley 94546

G. T. Sakai Co.
1313 Broadway, Sacramento 95818

K. Sakai Co.
1656 Post St., San Francisco 94115

Santos Market
245 E. Taylor St., San Jose 95112

Sell Rite Market 2
Lockford & Ham Lane, Lodi 95240

Senator Fish Market
2215 10th St., Sacramento 95818

Star Fish Market
320 S. Eldorado St., Stockton 95203

Stop-N-Shop Inc. Market
5815 Stockton Blvd.,
Sacramento 95820

Sunrise Grocery
299 E. Franklin St., Monterey 93940

Takahashi Co.
221 S. Claremont St.,
San Mateo 94401

Three Star Market
245 Washington St., Monterey 93940

Toyo Imports
815 Broadway, Seaside 93955

Westgate Lodi Super Market
311 S. Lower Sacramento, Lodi 95240

FRESNO AREA

Boys Market
1444 "C" St., Fresno 93706

Central Fish Co.
1507 Kern St., Fresno 93706

Fresno Fish Co.
919 "F" St., Fresno 93706

LOS ANGELES AREA

Alpha Beta Market #129
1500 W. Willow, Long Beach 90810

Alpha Beta Market #132
2740 W. Olympic Blvd.,
Los Angeles 90006

Aloha Grocery
4515 Centinela, Los Angeles 90066

Boys Market #5
3670 Crenshaw Blvd.,
Los Angeles 90016

Enbun Co.
248 E. 1st St., Los Angeles 90012

Food Co. #13
15505 S. Normandie, Gardena 90247

Hughes Market #9
11361 W. National Blvd.,
West Los Angeles 90064

Hughes Market #15
330 N. Atlantic Blvd.,
Monterey Park 91754

Ida Co.
339 E. 1st St., Los Angeles 90012

Japan Food Corp.
1131 Mateo St., Los Angeles 90021

Lucky Store #435
110 E. Carson St., Torrance 90502

Lucky Store #446
182nd & Western Ave.,
Torrance 90504

Meiji Market
1569 W. Redondo Beach Blvd.,
Gardena 90247

Modern Food Market
318 E. 2nd St., Los Angeles 90012

Oriental Food Market
1741 W. Willard, Long Beach 90810

Rafu Bussan Co.
344 E. 1st St., Los Angeles 90012

Safeway Store #107
4th & Soto St., Los Angeles 90033

Shi's Fish Market
9896 Garden Grove Blvd.,
Garden Grove 92640

Spot Market
15212 W. Western, Gardena 90249

Vons Grocery #43
5895 Lincoln Ave., Buena Park 90620

Woo Chee Chang
633 16th St., San Diego 92101

Yamasaki Market
1564 Santa Fe Ave., Long Beach 90813

COLORADO

Granada Fish Market
1275 19th St., Denver 80304

Pacific Mercantile Co.
1946 Larimer St., Denver 80202

Tandy's Pier 1 Imports
798 S. Santa Fe, Denver 80223

Tang's Imports
1600 28th St., Boulder 80301

Tang's Imports
3755 Cherry Creek N. Drive,
Denver 80209

Tang's Imports
10405 W. Colfax Ave.,
Lakewood 80215

FLORIDA

Fujiya Japanese Market
27960 S.W. 127th St.,
Homestead 33030

Oriental Imports
54 N. Orange Ave., Orlando 32801

Schiller's Delicatessen
3417 S. Manhattan Ave.,
Tampa 33609

Tropi Pac Food Products
3663 N.W. 47th St., Miami 33142

GEORGIA

Asian Trading Co., Ltd.

2581 Piedmont Rd.N.E.,
Atlanta 30324

Oriental Bazaar
262 E. Pacesferry Rd., Atlanta 30305

Oriental Food Gift Center
1351 Northside Drive N.W.,
Atlanta 30318

Oriental Food Market
2920 Dean Bridge Rd.,
Augusta 30904

IDAHO

Jim's Service & Gift
209 N. W. Main, Blackfoot 83221

Yuko's Gift
688 N. Holmes Ave.,
Idaho Falls 83401

ILLINOIS

Diamond Trading
1108 N. Clark St., Chicago 60610

Franklin Food Store
1309 E. 53rd St., Chicago 60609

Japan Food Corp.
1850 W. 43rd St., Chicago 60609

S & I Grocery
1058 W. Argyle St., Chicago 60640

Toguri Mercantile
5358 N. Clark St., Chicago 60657

INDIANA

Atlas Super Market
720 E. 54th St., Indianapolis 46220

Fuji's Gift & Foods
1401 E. Markland Ave.,
Kokomo 46901

Hatch's IGA Foodliner
1711 N. College St.,
Bloomington 47401

IOWA

Whiteway Super Market
212 S. Clinton St., Iowa City 52240

KANSAS

Cannon Market
201 Commercial St., Emporia 66801

Dyers Oriental Foods
505 W. 57th St., Topeka 66609

Imported Foods
1038 McCormick, Wichita 67213

Jade East
1000 Grant Ave., Junction City 66441

M & T Oriental Delicacies
1203 S. 2nd St., Leavenworth 66048

Toyo-ten Oriental Market
2744 California Ave., Topeka 66605

KENTUCKY

Oriental Food Store
850 N. Dixie Blvd., Radcliff 40160

LOUISIANA

Oriental Trading Co.
2636 Edenborn Ave., Metairie 70002

MARYLAND

Aberdeen Sweet Shop Bakery
6 S. Philadelphia Blvd.,
Aberdeen 20606

Japan Food Corp.
9179 Red Branch Rd., Columbia 21043

Japanese Shop
3708 Philadelphia Ave.,
Ocean City 21842

Oriental Boutique
Georgetown Alley, Laurel 20810

Zion Oriental Food
3717 Greenmount Ave.,
Baltimore 21218

MASSACHUSETTS

H. Schaffer & Co.
1714 Westover Rd., Chicopee 01020

Yoshinoya
36 Prospect St., Cambridge 02129

MICHIGAN

Mt. Fuji Oriental Foods & Gifts
22040 W. 10 Mile Rd.,
South Field 48075

Kuwahara Trading
Post 3126, Cass Ave., Detroit 48201

MINNESOTA

Golden Star Manufacturing Co.
2426 E. 26th St., Minneapolis 55406

International House
712 Washington Ave. S.E.,
Minneapolis 55414

MISSOURI

Aloha Enterprises
1741 Swope Parkway,
Kansas City 64110

Maruyama's
100 N. 18th St., St. Louis 63103

Won's Oriental Imports
821 E. Broadway, Columbia 65201

NEBRASKA

Oriental Trading Co.
1115 Farnam St., Omaha 68113

NEVADA

Nevada Sea Food Co.
345 E. 2nd St., Reno 89501

Oriental Food of Las Vegas
25 E. Oakey Blvd., Las Vegas 89105

NEW JERSEY

Haruko's Oriental Bazaar
Rt. 3, Box 3143, Browns Mills 08015

Kabuki
9 E. Main St., Columbus 08022

Miyako Oriental Foods
490 Main St., Fort Lee 07024

Seabrook Village Store
E. Parsonage Rd., Seabrook 08302

NEW YORK

AC Gift
2642 Central Ave., Yonkers 10710

Cho Sun Kim Co.
407 Central Ave., Albany 12206

East Food Store
74–15 Woodside Ave., Elmhurst 11373

Far East Food & Gift Center
43–05 48th St., Sunnyside 11104

Japan Food Corp.
11–31 31st Ave.,
Long Island City 11106

Japan Mart, Inc.
239 W. 105th St., New York 10025

Japanese Foodland
2620 Broadway, New York 10025

Katagiri & Co.
224 E. 59th St., New York 10022

Main Street Foods, Inc.
41–54 Main St., Flushing 11355

Marumiya Co.
318–320 W. 231 St., Bronx 10463

Mitsuba Co., Inc.
59–10 92nd St., Elmhurst 11372

Nippon Do
82–69 Parsons Blvd., Jamaica 11432

OK Specialties
101 Mohawk Ave., Scotia 12302

Oriental Food Shop
1302 Amsterdam Ave.,
New York 10027

The Oriental Shop
203 N. Aurora St., Ithaca 14850

Tanaka & Co.
326 Amsterdam Ave.,
New York 10023

Tsujimoto Oriental Art & Gift
6530 Seneca St., Elma 14059

NORTH CAROLINA

Fujii Food Co.
1405 Hope Mills Rd.,
Fayetteville 29304

Gourmet Center Inc.
1004 W. Main St., Durham 27701

Oriental Food Mart
803 N. Main St. (P.O. Box 202),
Spring Lake 28390

IHIO

Dayton Oriental Food Store
812 Xenia Ave., Dayton 45410

Ida Oriental Foods & Gifts
614 Yearling Rd., Columbus 43213

Omura Japanese Food & Gift Shop
3811 Payne Ave., Cleveland 44114

Soya Food Products
2356 Wyoming Ave.,
Cincinnati 45214

OKLAHOMA

Fuji-san Oriental Foods
3008 N.W. 28th St.,
Oklahoma City 73107

OREGON

Anzen Importers
736 N.E. Union Ave.,
Portland 97232

Ontario Market
203 Idaho Ave., Ontario 97914

Soy Bean Products Co.
336 S. W. 5th St., Ontario 97914

PENNSYLVANIA

Arirang House
4516 Baltimore Ave.,
Philadelphia 19104

Bando Trading Co.
2126 Murray Ave., Pittsburgh 15217

Oriental Food Mart
909 Race St., Philadelphia 19107

Oriental Food Store
318 Atwood St., Pittsburgh 15213

Tokyo Imports
329 Market St., Harrisburg 17101

TENNESSEE

Barrizizza Brothers Inc.
351–353 S. Front St.,
Memphis 38103

Northtown Big Star Market
2501 Clarksville Highway,
Nashville 37208

The Orient
1513 Church St., Nashville 37203

TEXAS

Japan Food Corp.
2002½ White St., Houston 77010

Tachibana Co.
4886 Hercules Ave., E1 Paso 76102

UTAH

Sage Farm Market
52 W. 1st S. St., Salt Lake City 84102

VIRGINIA

Ann Kiji Shop
Cronin Festherstone Mai,
Woodbridge 22191

Chinese American Trading Co.
313 Resevoir Ave., Norfolk 23504

Suzukas Oriental Food Store
145 W. Ocean View Ave.,
Norfolk 23503

Vaughans Esso Station
17423 Warwick Blvd.,
Newport News 23607

Yamas Orient Food & Gifts
21 S. Mallery St., Hampton 23503

WASHINGTON

M K Fish Market & Grocery
1800 E. Yesler Way, Seattle 98122

North Coast Importing
515 Maynard Ave., Seattle 98104

North Coast Supply Co.
27th Main Ave., Spokane 99201

Pier 1 Imports
13250 Aurora Ave. N.,
Seattle 98133

Tobo Co.
504 12th Ave. S., Seattle 98144

Uwajimaya Co.
6th Ave. S. & S. King St.,
Seattle 98104

Uwajimaya Co.
South Center Shopping Hall,
Tukwila 98188

WASHINGTON, D. C.

House of Hanna
1468 "T" St., N.W. 20009

Mikado
4709 Wisconsin Ave., N.W. 20016

WEST VIRGINIA

George Enterprises
374 Patterson Dr., Morgantown 26305

WISCONSIN

International House of Foods
440 W. Gorham, Madison 53704

Oriental Grocery & Gift
821 N. 27th St., Milwaukee 53208

Topitzes
4401 Lisbon Ave., Milwaukee 53208

WYOMING

Fuji Food Inc.
4007 Warren Ave., Cheyenne 82001

CANADA

Furuya Trading Ltd.
460 Dundas W., Toronto, Ontario

Marufuji Trading Co., Ltd.
P.O. Box 3631, Vancouver, B. C.

Shimizu Shoten
356 Powell St., Vancouver, B. C.

List of Recipes by Nation

China

Japan

Korea

Philippine Islands

Indonesia and Southeast Asia

Indonesia

Southeast Asia

India

Iran

The Levant

Syria

Turkey

Greece

Index of Selected Ingredients

ham 85, 139
harusame 85, 153
hazelnuts 169
hot roll mix 189

kampyo 105
katsuobushi(shavings of dried
    bonito) 69
kelp 69

lamb 37, 159, 161, 167, 169, 175,
    185, 186, 190
lemon 164
lentils 122, 168
lime 164
lotus root 85, 107

mackerel 79
matsutake mushrooms 103
mussels 182
mutton 45, 144, 158, 159

okra 150, 176
onions 27, 45, 187, 188
oysters 94, 98, 121

pea pods 150
pearl barley 125
peas 162
phylo pastry 184
pineapple 24, 163
pistachio nuts 169
pompano 79
pork 25, 26, 28, 33, 36, 39, 40, 41,
    44, 45, 49, 52-55, 59, 80, 89, 90,
    128, 138, 158, 161
pork liver 24
pork loin 81
potatos 86, 163
prawns 31, 86, 87, 98, 123, 148, 152
pulwal 150
pumpkin seeds 169

red kidney beans 122
red snapper 29, 30
rice 63-65, 111-116,
    118-121, 123, 125, 126, 143, 187,
    188
rice, glutinous 28, 65, 122, 123,
    145
rice, long-grain 63, 172
rice, pulverized 183

salmon 49
sardines 79
sea bream 92, 98
shiitake mushrooms 21, 41, 45, 59,
    86, 98, 106, 120, 134, 179
short ribs 132
shrimp 23, 44, 52, 53, 85-87, 102,
    108
sirloin 34, 35, 99, 129
snow peas 21
sole 30
spinach 35, 76, 90
squid 108, 192
summer squash 175
sweet potatos 85, 86
sweet rice flour 140

taro root 98, 155
tenderloin 129
trout 146
tuna 50, 94
turnips 77, 134

udon noodles 100

venison 45
vermicelli 85, 153

walnuts 170
watermelon seeds 169
wheat, cracked 183
whitefish 29, 30